# The Word From The Wise Old Woman

## Sermons From A Feminine Perspective

### Nancy Bauer-King

CSS Publishing Company, Inc., Lima, Ohio

Scripture quotations are from the *New Revised Standard Version of the Bible*, copyright
1989 by the Division of Christian Education of the National Council of the Churches of
Christ in the USA. Used by permission.

**Library of Congress Cataloging-in-Publication Data**

Bauer-King, Nancy, 1940-
     The word from the wise old woman : sermons from a feminine perspective / Nancy
Bauer-King.
        p.    cm.
     ISBN 0-7880-1293-2 (alk. paper)
     1. United Methodist Church (U.S.)—Sermons. 2. Sermons, American—Women au-
thors. 3. Story sermons. I. Title.
BX8333.B43W67        1998
252'.076—dc21                                                                            98-9665
                                                                                             CIP

ISBN 0-7880-1293-2

*To Charles*

# Table of Contents

Foreword                                            7

The Parable Of The Wise Old Woman                  11
  *Matthew 21:28-32*

The Wise Old Woman Sees                            19
  *Mark 10:46-52*

The Impractical Wise Old Woman                     25
  *John 12:1-8*

The Wise Old Woman's Thanksgiving                  31
  *Luke 17:11-19*

The Wise Old Woman Says Good-bye                   37
  *Matthew 9:35—10:8*

The Wise Old Woman Walks On Water                  43
  *Matthew 14:22-33*

The Touch Of The Wise Old Woman                    49
  *Mark 5:21-43*

The Wise Old Woman Goes Fishing                    57
  *Luke 5:1-11*

The Wise Old Woman Watch                           63
  *Luke 12:32-40; Jeremiah 18:1-11*

The Wise Old Woman Intrudes                        69
  *Genesis 9:8-17; Mark 1:9-15*

The Wise Old Woman On The Loose                    75
  *John 14:15-31*

The Wise Old Woman Straight                                  81
    *Jeremiah 1:4-10; Luke 13:10-17*

A Choosy Wise Old Woman                                      87
    *Deuteronomy 30:15-20; Matthew 5:21-26*

# Foreword

It was early September in that once-upon-a-time place in the southeast corner of the state whose thumb sticks out like a hitchhiker into Lake Michigan. A pastor, who had recently been reappointed to a church near that same lake, was anxious. A collection of her sermons had been accepted for publication and she was eyeballing a deadline. Everything was finished and ready for print except the foreword.

The sermons, stories which were conversations between the pastor and a Wise Old Woman, had been preached over a ten-year period to people she knew. How would she introduce the Wise Old Woman to folks she *didn't* know?

"Aha!" she thought with sudden insight. "I'll consult the Wise Old Woman herself for an answer," and she was soon sipping coffee with her friend at their favorite restaurant.

After explaining her deadline and dilemma with the foreword, the pastor and the Wise Old Woman had the following conversation:

"What do I say about you, Wise Old Woman?"

"Why do you have to say *anything*?"

"Well, over the years I've been telling these stories, lots of people have asked about you. They want to know who you are."

"Who do you say I am?"

"I never know exactly *how* to answer. I usually get a goofy grin on my face."

"So, why do you need to explain *now*?"

"Well, Mr. Lentz, my editor, thought it would help readers if you were set in context."

"Hmmm. Better context than concrete. I suppose people do want their intellects satisfied. What did you tell Mr. Lentz?"

"I thought you might ask me that. I brought this paragraph I wrote to him as we were discussing the book's title. Here's what I said:"

*In addition to being an archetypal figure, the Wise Old Woman is a metaphor for God's immanent presence with me. She is an inner voice with whom I hold council. Sermons in this volume are stories which have resulted from such dialogue. The story, as it unfolds, reveals the Good News of the Gospel — at least to me. If there were a muse for the exegetical-hermeneutical process, the Wise Old Woman would be such a muse.*

"My, oh my. I guess our experiences *are* a-musing, aren't they?"

"Yes. They're delightful to me. Much more than that, they're transformative. You provide safe space for me, silent and soft as a womb from which words are born. You are like a midwife helping me to bring the words of Good News to birth once again. I remember our first conversation, how stuck I was and lost. My divorce had been final for only two months and I'd just returned from helping my younger daughter and her husband bury their first child. How could I preach GOOD news on Sunday? And, then, there YOU were!"

"Thank you, my dear. You asked for help, you know."

"Oh, another issue. I want to apologize to you, Wise Old Woman, for not consulting you before putting you in print."

"It's quite all right, my dear. Your sermons are 'thank-yous,' really. They point to God's presence with us. And, as you know, people make their own interpretations of what they read. What *is* your hope by sharing these private conversations?"

"I hope there will be an opening and expansion of images and metaphors for God. For too many years the only image of God I had was 'father.' I tried to relate to a God who was stern, demanding, punitive, and meted out love only as a reward for being perfect. I never measured up. One of my pastors helped when he shared this slogan: 'Not to call God "Father" is unbiblical. To call God only "Father" is idolatry.' I hope people will see God's grace can be revealed through anything. Especially old women. Old women in our culture are often poor, ignored, denigrated, and rendered useless. Or worse, a burden. I just realized, I don't even know your name, Wise Old Woman. Is it Sophie?"

"My name is not important. More important to you are the names of those people who have embodied God's love to you."

"Yes ..."

"Who are they?"

"There are dozens. Young and old. There's Rusty. Brenda. Hazelyn. Gerry. Linda. Inez. Bessie. Phoebe. Margaret. Pam. Julie. Jill. Karen. Emily. Gayle. Sara. Shirley. Jane. Rosemary. Joyce. Sharon. Jean. Mimi. Susanne. And Alice-at-Ragdale-Foundation, who gave me sacred space, too."

"Aren't there any men?"

"Oh, yes! Charlie. Thad. Paul. Jack. Bruce. Wesley. Bill. Russell. Phil. Steve. Jerry. Jim. Dave. And children, too! Becky. Bobby. Brian. Alex. Tommy. Andrew. Maranda. Kalyn. Kelsey. Kendall. Cody. Carson. Brett. John. Adam. Erik."

"WOW! What a list!"

"There are more ... I haven't even begun to list folks in the congregations I served, the people who listened to your words as well as mine. When I picture these folks, my heart is full of gratitude!"

"Another wise old woman once said that not to be able to give one's gifts to those whom one loves most is the only real deprivation in life. The stories of our conversations are gifts you offer, my dear. But what about the foreword? What words will you say?"

"I don't know, Wise Old Woman, but since this conversation, I'm not anxious about it anymore. I'm sure I'll think of something."

And with that, the two friends left the restaurant, each going their separate way into a bright, beautiful fall day.

Nancy Bauer-King
September 4, 1997

9

# The Parable Of The Wise Old Woman

## Matthew 21:28-32

*Once upon a time* on a Friday morning in late September, a pastor, serving a two-point charge in the northeast portion of an upper Midwest state whose thumb sticks up into Lake Michigan, woke up.

The first thing the pastor thought of was the dream she had just been having. It was about a waitress named Spiceina. The pastor had just given Spiceina a five-dollar tip for a cup of coffee and, in the dream, the hostess of the restaurant was chasing the pastor with the five dollars trying to give it back to her. The pastor was saying to the hostess, "Waitressing is hard work with low pay. Spiceina has four children to feed ..."

The pastor woke up as the hostess was heading toward the kitchen waving the five dollars and hollering, "Spicy ... Spicy ..."

The second thing the pastor thought of was the sermon for Sunday. It wasn't even started. She'd thought about the scripture all week, but still didn't have any words down. She tried to go back to sleep and couldn't. She decided that this morning was one of those times she'd have to go ask the Wise Old Woman for advice.

Seventeen minutes later, the pastor found herself in the back corner of the French Town Custard Restaurant where the outrageous Wise Old Woman hangs out drinking coffee, painting her long fingernails neon colors, and polishing her rings.

"So," said the Wise Old Woman, talking loudly to be heard over the speaker tuned in to WIXX, which was blaring out a song about the NFL strike called "Picket Line Shuffle."

11

"So, you're stuck again."

"Yes," said the pastor dejectedly and then explained, "I'm not stuck over what to say to the folks on Sunday morning so much as I am stuck *how* to say it. You see, the scripture is a parable. It is one of Jesus' *stories*. The Bible is full of a wide variety of writing: genealogies, battle accounts, laws, histories, poetry, measurements of arks! All of the writing, of course, is meant to point to God, but parables are unique. Jesus took a common, everyday situation, wove a story around it which got folks to think and ask questions about God, and then in conversation maybe discover an answer or two."

"What's the matter, Pastor?" asked the Wise Old Woman. "Can't you think of any examples? Sermon illustrations? Common stuff of the everyday life of your congregations?"

"On the contrary, Wise Old Woman. Jesus used a *very* common example easily applied to our lives. He tells about two men who are asked to make a decision to go to work. One man says, 'No, I won't go' — and then changes his mind and goes. The other man says the opposite: 'Sure, I'll go' — and then he doesn't.

"That behavior happens all the time," continued the pastor. "Sometimes I do it myself. I've got *lots* of examples. All week I've dealt with people saying 'Yes' or 'No' to invitations or responsibilities:

'No, I don't want to be on that committee.'

'Yes, I'll be at that meeting.'

'No, I'm not coming to Confirmation.'

"*Today*, Linda, Joe, Pearl, Norma, Shirley, and I are trying to get folks to go to our District Fall Celebration next week. Who knows by next Sunday *who* will actually get on the bus? Some people come. Some don't. *That's* not the problem."

The Wise Old Woman looked impatient. The pastor thought maybe she wanted to get back to painting her nails. The Wise Old Woman played with one of her rings and said, "Well, what *is* your problem, then?"

"Well, my problem isn't who shows up next Sunday. Whoever shows up represents the Body of Christ gathered, and God's presence is there. And my problem isn't with folks keeping their word. Most people, when they say they'll be somewhere, are there. And, if they can't make it, they call. I mean ... things change in people's lives ... folks get sick ... some get tired."

"Some folks get sick and tired," quipped the Wise Old Woman. The pastor wondered if the Wise Old Woman was getting sick and tired of *her*.

"So," the Wise Old Woman asked again, not trying to disguise her impatience, "The *problem*?"

The pastor stated her case.

"Well, Wise Old Woman, Jesus used this common situation story to point to God. *How* can I use the story to do the same? My job is to tell Good News in such a way that folks' relationship with God is made stronger. *How* can I do that?"

"Oh," said the Wise Old Woman, sitting up a little straighter and becoming a little more interested now that the problem was clearly defined. "Where *is* the Good News in this parable?"

"That's where it gets tricky to explain," answered the pastor.

"Jesus told the story to all sorts of Jewish people. Some were outcasts, some sinners, some stiff-necked self-righteous religious officials. Some were sick, some were tired ... some were sick and tired.

"In this story, Jesus points to the ministry of John the Baptist and seems to be saying that the folks listening to John are getting into the Kingdom of God before the religious establishment people."

The Wise Old Woman continued the flow of conversation.

"And John? What was his ministry?"

The pastor answered directly out of New Testament 101.

"Well, John was saying, 'Repent.' That meant 'just turn around.' Turn from participating in destructive things and turn back toward God. That implies that the folks didn't have to be church members or officials. That implies that folks didn't have to live out a bunch of rules to be in God's Kingdom."

The Wise Old Woman shrugged her shoulders, stretched out her hands in a gesture which indicated the problem was solved, and said, "So, there it is. Say to the people: *'Turn toward God. Go to the vineyard.'*"

"Sure," said the pastor, who liked complexity and good dialogue. "It still isn't that simple. Matthew (who wrote this story) wrote it *after* Jesus had died and *after* the amazing claim that Jesus was resurrected. Matthew wasn't writing it to Jewish folks only. He was writing to Gentiles as well."

"Oh, I see," said the Wise Old Woman. And, she quickly demonstrated her wisdom with a remark that proved she *did*, indeed, see: "You're saying the same story said to different people may have a different meaning to the hearers. Depending upon their situation, folks may look at the same story in different ways."

"Yes," replied the pastor. "Matthew took many of Jesus' stories and arranged them in such a way that certain points were made. In this case, Matthew put the story with a couple of other parables which have the intention of proving Jesus' authority. By Matthew's time, the story of Christ's death and resurrection was spreading throughout the area: to Jews, Gentiles, everyone. The question for folks to decide was, 'Who *is* this man, Jesus? God's son? The Messiah?' The question for folks was, 'Is what Jesus said about God *true*? If so, what does that mean for *my* life?'

"Oh, Wise Old Woman," continued the pastor, "My problem is the folks I preach to are baptized. They *already* say they believe in Christ as the Son of God and have turned toward God. With regard to the Kingdom of God, they are folks like the second son in the parable. Each one, by being baptized, has already said, 'Yes, I'll go. Yes, I'll work in God's vineyard world.' "

Now the light dawned on the face of the Wise Old Woman. She knew this pastor very well.

"I see your problem, honey. You're afraid of the second part of the equation of the second son. The conclusion. The son in the parable says, 'Yes, I'll go,' and he doesn't. You're worried because you wonder if that means that conclusion is also the one to be drawn on Sunday morning. You're afraid to put that question before the folks. You're afraid the scripture is requiring you to say, 'Look, folks — you've promised to work in God's world. How are you doing?' And you're afraid the folks will infer that you don't think they're doing very well. And you are very uncomfortable calling folks to be accountable to their promises."

The Wise Old Woman sighed deeply and, as her chest expanded, the pastor noticed for the first time that the Wise Old Woman had on an outrageous purple sweatshirt decorated with sequins, rhinestones, and sparkling beads. With astonishment, the pastor noticed the glitter spelled out the Wise Old Woman's initials: W.O.W. WOW!

Across the front of the Wise Old Woman, the *word* WOW!

As the pastor was contemplating this amazing connection, the Wise Old Woman spoke.

"In reality, honey, even the parables don't contain the *whole* truth. There are at least two other options not even mentioned in this story. There are two sons, right? The son who says he'll go and doesn't and the son who says he won't and does?

"What about the other two options which immediately come to mind? A son who says, 'No, I won't go' and doesn't, and a son who says, 'Yes, I will go' — and *does*.

"What's the bottom line in this parable, honey? What does Jesus want to communicate above all else? That God wants folks in the vineyard kingdom. God wants all people to love God and each other and creation. That is a truth for *all* time for *all* people."

The Wise Old Woman, having made her point, looked at the pastor and asked, "Who are the folks you'll be preaching to Sunday morning?"

Faces of the folks in the two congregations flashed in front of the pastor's face. She watched with tenderness for a moment and then answered, "Well, they are people who struggle with life. Who try. Who trust each other — sometimes. Who have survived tragedies. Who care for each other as best as they can. They are folks who are busy, who work hard, who are sick ... and tired. They are the sons and daughters of God who have said, 'Yes, we want to be in God's Kingdom. We believe Christ's promise of love and we want to go where we'll receive it.' "

The sunlight coming through the window of the restaurant hit the Wise Old Woman's sweatshirt in such a way that the reflection off the WOW shed an even further insight in the pastor's mind.

"Ah, I see. We church folk have already said, 'Yes,' like the second son. A question to consider is, 'Are we or are we not at work in God's vineyard? Are we or are we not in God's presence?' "

The Wise Old Woman nodded and gently said, "And, who did Christ say was getting in *first*?"

"The tax collectors and prostitutes," quickly answered the pastor, hoping that the Wise Old Woman wouldn't ask her about the behavior of the folks gathered on Sunday morning.

But instead, the Wise Old Woman acted as if the behavior wasn't the issue at all. She asked,

"Why did Jesus say those folks get in first?" And the Wise Old Woman answered her own question, her initials gleaming silver and gold. "Jesus didn't say they'd get in *because* of their behavior. He said they'd get in because they knew they weren't perfect and knew how desperately they needed God. They knew how much they longed to be in the vineyard. What does that say to you, honey? You — who comes to me afraid and broken, too?"

Now the pastor was feeling like a child. She listened as the Wise Old Woman loved her and gave *her* Good News:

"It's not the folks like the Pharisees who are in God's presence. It's not the folks who think they know all the right words or how to do the right sermon. It's not the folks who think they know the religious rules and are rigidly and self-righteously and *joylessly* living them out.

"The folks who get into God's Kingdom vineyard are the folks who know they're not perfect. The folks who are afraid, the folks who are hurt, the folks who feel guilt, who agonize over broken relationships ... the folks who are sick ... and tired ... and sick and tired. The folks who are acutely aware of the separation from God. It's the folks who say, 'Yes. I'll go into the vineyard and work with God. There's *nothing* which could keep me away!'

"It's the folks who not only go, but while they're there, they are the folks who will be making wine, and when the work is done, they'll drink that sweet flowing wine with their brothers and sisters ... communion."

The pastor, subdued, was barely able to let herself breathe and barely able to let herself feel the love this Wise Old Woman offered.

"So," she whispered, "what should I say on Sunday morning?"

"Just remind folks of the choice they have. They've already said one 'Yes.' Ask them to consider prayerfully if they have said or are saying the second 'Yes.' If they're not sure, simply invite them to do so."

The pastor, lost in thought, still trying to figure out *how* to tell Jesus' story, didn't notice the Wise Old Woman was gone until the waitress came to fill her coffee cup. Seeing the waitress reminded the pastor of her dream, the outrageous tip she had given to Spiceina — a waitress working hard at low pay to raise four kids.

The pastor got up. Figuring that any waitress who would keep the coffee cups of two weird women filled was worth a lot of money, she left an outrageous tip on the table and headed to her office to figure out *how* to preach the parable on Sunday morning.

# The Wise Old Woman Sees

## Mark 10:46-52

*Once again upon a* time, the pastor serving that two-point charge up above where the thumb of Wisconsin sticks out into Lake Michigan like a hitchhiker woke up.

It was 4:45 a.m. Still dark. She had a headache. It was Friday morning and the sermon for Sunday was not even begun. The pastor was particularly nervous about this sermon because it would be videotaped and reviewed by a group of her clergy colleagues.

The scripture the pastor was to preach on was the story about blind Bartimaeus. She'd preached that text before and nothing new was being shown to her. As this headachy pastor stumbled through the dark hallway to the bathroom, she felt like Bartimaeus.

"I'm blind, too," she thought. "At least about this sermon. I have no in-sight. I have no out-sight, either."

The pastor amused herself with plays on words.

"And, out-a-sight is where I'd like to be on Sunday morning."

As the pastor turned on the bathroom light and saw herself in the mirror, she decided it was time to head over to French Town Custard. Her reflection agreed, "Yes, it's time to find the Wise Old Woman."

This time the pastor found the Wise Old Woman sitting in the darkest corner of the restaurant. She was dressed all in black. She had a cup of coffee in front of her and was busily painting her fingernails. Yellow.

"She looks more like a Halloween witch than a Wise Old Woman," the pastor thought as she approached the shadowy figure.

Remembering the last time she'd seen the Wise Old Woman —
the way the sunlight had gleamed off the initials W.O.W. on her
rhinestone-studded sweatshirt (WOW!) — the pastor despaired of
any light being shed this morning. It was all too, too dark.

As the pastor greeted her friend, the Wise Old Woman put down
the nail polish, blew on her nails, and took a sip of coffee.

"I haven't seen you for a while, pastor. Been doing it all on
your own, then?"

The pastor wondered if the Wise Old Woman meant the words
as a sarcastic reference to the pastor's difficulty in asking for help
when she needed it. The pastor wanted to protest. Her clergy
brothers and sisters had spent a couple of hours together looking at
and talking about this scripture. The pastor knew she *had* asked
for help, but she wasn't here to defend herself. She decided to
ignore the Wise Old Woman's comment. She pulled out a chair,
sat down, and quickly got to the problem.

"Wise Old Woman, I need help again with my sermon."

"Aha. You're stuck?"

"Blind is more like it. I just can't see anything in the scripture
story — at least anything that clicks with *me*."

"Oh? What's the story?"

"It's an old story. Another of Jesus' healings. This healing is
of a blind beggar named Bartimaeus. I've done my reading and
have gathered all sorts of information."

The pastor began sharing what she'd learned.

"Jesus is passing through Jericho on his way to Jerusalem. It's
pass-OVER time. Pilgrims are heading to the Temple for the an-
nual religious celebrations and offerings. Lots of priests who tend
the Temple live in Jericho. So the large crowd gathered would be
full of pilgrims and priests. It was a good crowd. Lots of opportunity for a beggar."

The Wise Old Woman, picking at a cuticle, didn't seem to be
too interested in the pastor's commentary. She interrupted, "Do
you think people gathered on Sunday morning to worship are interested in all those facts?"

"I don't know. Maybe ..." answered the pastor. "But it's probably not where their GREATEST interest is."

(One of the pastor's greatest interests was early morning coffee, and just then the waitress appeared with a nice fresh cup.)

The pastor turned to thank the waitress, but the Wise Old Woman continued her inquiry.

"Well, what do you think the people's greatest interest IS?"

"The miracle," the pastor answered, confidently. "The miracle. Bartimaeus being healed. I think all people long for some miracle or other in their lives. Whether it's blindness, cancer, arthritis, painful memories, loneliness, starvation ... I think we all have something we want healed."

The Wise Old Woman began rubbing her hip with her yellow-tipped fingers as if the pastor's words had reminded her of hidden aches and pains. She made a gesture of impatience and said, "Well, Pastor, let's look at the miracle part of the story more closely. What *exactly* happened?"

The pastor, eager to display her research, responded, "Bartimaeus hears Jesus is near. He sets up a fuss, insisting that he be heard by Jesus. Bystanders — probably pilgrims and priests — scold him. Beggars and physically impaired people weren't allowed access to the Temple. Why should he be allowed access to Jesus?"

The Wise Old Woman broke into the recital. "To speak up for himself against that kind of social pressure must have taken a great deal of courage!"

"Yes," the pastor agreed. "Self-esteem. Assertiveness training. That sort of thing. Or maybe Bartimaeus was just plain obnoxious. In any case, he insisted loudly that he wanted Jesus' mercy. And Jesus heard him and asked him, 'What do you want me to do for you?'

"Now here's where the story gets interesting, Wise Old Woman," the pastor continued. "Jesus didn't seem to DO anything. Bartimaeus simply told Jesus he wanted his sight and Jesus said, 'Your faith has made you well.' Just like that, Bartimaeus could see again!"

"Hmmm ..." mused the Wise Old Woman. "Jesus didn't do ANYTHING?"

"Well, he listened to Bartimaeus. He didn't reject him. He asked him what he wanted. But then he told him he already had it. Confusing, huh?"

"How do you mean confusing, my dear?"

The pastor, thinking of the people who would be worshiping with her on Sunday morning, answered, "I talk to folks all the time who long for miracles. They say what they want. They have faith, too. But there's no guarantee there will be a miracle."

"That must be difficult for you," sympathized the Wise Old Woman.

The pastor felt good being listened to. Being understood by the Wise Old Woman was comforting somehow.

"Yes, it is difficult," the pastor responded. "I care about the people I pastor. I care about myself. I know there's something we all want God to do for us, and I know God wants wholeness for all of us. But my caring is not enough. God is in charge of the miracle department. And when we don't get what we want, a frustrating stand-off occurs."

The Wise Old Woman considered the pastor's words and then said, "Might part of the wisdom of this story be in WHAT we want?"

"How do you mean?"

The Wise Old Woman looked at her yellow nails and said, "I'm thinking of your clergy friend, Bob. When you clergy were gathered and all working on this passage, I liked Bob's insight. Do you remember it? He said, 'For years that blind beggar had sat by the side of the road asking for money. But money wasn't what he REALLY wanted. What he REALLY wanted was his sight. Bartimaeus didn't ask Jesus for money. He asked him for his SIGHT.' "

The pastor was stunned by the Wise Old Woman's remarks. It wasn't Bob's insight. She remembered that, too. The pastor wondered how the Wise Old Woman knew what was said at the clergy group. However, the pastor couldn't explore that amazing question at the moment because she had a more important question to ask.

"You mean, Wise Old Woman, that WHAT we ask for is a crucial part of God's answer?"

"Perhaps. The story seems to suggest that. Let's try it out. What about YOU, my dear?"

"Me?"

"Yes. Why did you come looking for me this morning? What do you want me to do for you?"

The question sounded vaguely familiar. The pastor replied, "I don't know."

"You'll have to do better than that, Pastor. Jesus asked that very question of Bartimaeus, and the blind man KNEW what he wanted."

The pastor was nonplused. She began to answer tentatively, "I came to you because I was blind ... I wanted help with my sermon."

"What kind of help?"

"I don't know."

The Wise Old Woman pushed. "Did you want me to do it FOR you?"

The pastor was beginning to catch on. She remembered the quote she had seen recently: GOD GIVES US THE BOAT AND OARS, BUT WE HAVE TO ROW. She looked straight at the Wise Old Woman and answered, "No. I don't want you to do the sermon for me. Jesus didn't SEE for the blind man. God has called *me* to preach ... to tell the good news of healing love the way I see it. What I want from you, Wise Old Woman, is to help me see the way I see it. I want you to help me see what I already know within."

And, at that moment, the sun split a huge black cloud, rushed through the restaurant window, and hit the brightest things in the place — the Wise Old Woman's yellow fingernails. There was a brief glitter as the pastor said softly, "I want in-sight. I want to see what God sees. I want to see God."

The Wise Old Woman remained silent for a few moments, studying her nails. Then, seeing a spot she had missed, she picked up the polish and said, "Did you catch on to something, my dear?"

"I think so," the pastor nodded. But she also knew in-sight is elusive. God doesn't show Godself easily. She hurried to capture the truth she had seen.

"I can't get a hold of it exactly, Wise Old Woman. But I think of Jesus. How he talked about the Kingdom of God within us. How he promised that God is always present and we just can't see. We baptized people have trouble seeing God within ourselves and each other. And, I think of Bartimaeus. He literally wanted to see God. SEE Jesus. And, what Jesus did was to help him see what he already saw deep within himself. His seeing his faith was all Bartimaeus needed. Perhaps we all want to see our faith — God within us. When we do, maybe we'll be whole, too."

The Wise Old Woman showed her wisdom by once again remaining silent. But the pastor continued reflecting. "I seemed to SEE when I clearly said what I wanted. Like Bartimaeus, God must want my in-sight, too."

The Wise Old Woman's only reaction was a gentle smile which crept across her face like a ray of sunshine.

"It was a nice moment for me," said the pastor softly. "Like a small miracle, here with you. I'm not sure it will help me with my sermon. Folks gather to hear GOOD NEWS. They want to hear words which promise them God's healing. I don't know if I'll have anything to say."

At this, the Wise Old Woman leaned back and folded her hands, which showed ten spots which seemed to shine like gold. With great tenderness she said, "I'm sure, my dear, that you'll think of something."

# The Impractical Wise Old Woman

## John 12:1-8

*It was once again* upon a time. Wednesday morning, March 8, 1989, to be exact. The pastor serving that two-point charge north of where the thumb of Wisconsin sticks out into Lake Michigan like a hitchhiker decided to go out for breakfast. She'd been up late the night before looking in vain for the aurora borealis, which the weatherman had promised. She was sitting in a booth at Wayne's Restaurant, removing the paper from a bran muffin, when she saw a familiar figure trudge in. It was the Wise Old Woman.

Now, some of you have met the Wise Old Woman. She is a strange person. She wears outlandish clothing and garish make-up and jewelry. Most often she is seen in a purple sweatshirt with her initials in rhinestones across the front. She most often appears just when the pastor is stuck with a sermon and through conversation with the Wise Old Woman, the pastor receives insight.

This morning, however, the pastor did a double take. Her friend was bundled up in a blaze-orange snowsuit. And, as she reflected upon the status of her sermon for the upcoming Sunday, the pastor convinced herself she did not need anyone's help.

Just as she was wondering, "What is the Wise Old Woman doing at Wayne's?" the ersatz hunter turned and spied the pastor.

"Ah, Pastor. Good to see you. I've been *hunting* for you. I see you're alone. May I join you?"

The pastor, not used to the Wise Old Woman seeking *her* out, was taken off guard. But the Wise Old Woman was already seating herself, and so the pastor nodded her head in assent.

25

"I do not like the way your sermon is going, my dear," said the Wise Old Woman, getting right to the point.

"WHAT?" responded the pastor. With a flooding mixture of shock at the directness of her visitor, and sinking fear that all her work so far this week was about to go down the drain, the pastor did not even wonder *how* the Wise Old Woman knew what she was doing on the sermon.

Unzipping neon nylon, the Wise Old Woman continued her confrontation. "Isn't the scripture for Sunday John's account of Mary pouring nard over Jesus' feet?"

The pastor nodded. She had laughed to herself earlier about "nard" sounding like a cross between "nerd" and "lard." She grinned at the memory, but the Wise Old Woman didn't give her a chance to share her joke.

"You, my dear," the Wise Old Woman scolded, "are on the wrong track in your sermon. You are all taken up with Jesus' comment in the story about the poor. Remember? Jesus says something about always having the poor with you. Well, you are trying to make sense out of his comment. In the words of a hunter, you are missing the mark!"

"But, Wise Old Woman," objected the pastor, "Jesus spent his whole ministry helping the poor, ill, and outcast. This comment he makes is so unfeeling. Completely out of character. In fact, people sometimes quote him so they can excuse themselves from doing charity. I can't believe Jesus would say this."

"What you can't believe, Pastor, is that there is ever an occasion for abandoning practicality." The Wise Old Woman repeated more gently, "You can't believe there would ever be a time in which pouring out $15,000 worth of perfume (that's at today's prices) would be exactly the thing to do. Every bone in your body reeks of frugality, my dear." The pastor thought she heard the Wise Old Woman mumble "borderline miser" into her bright orange collar.

Upon quick reflection, the pastor agreed with the Wise Old Woman. She had been raised in a home in which every penny was counted and counted again. Sometimes there were not enough pennies. On the rare occasion when there was extra money — like when the choir surprised her father with a Christmas gift — the money was spent in a practical way. Groceries. A new pair of shoes. Kerosene for the burner. If nothing was immediately needed, the money was saved for a disaster. It was never spent for fun.

As if she was reading her mind, the Wise Old Woman asked, "Do you remember your high school friend, Mary?"

"Oh no," thought the pastor. "Another Mary? I'll never keep these names straight!"

The Wise Old Woman was insistent. "You remember. Mary's fiancé, Tom, came home on a two-week leave from the Air Force to attend his grandfather's funeral. While he was home — on the spur of the moment — Tom and Mary got married. Married on Friday and separated on Sunday when Tom had to return to Denver. You remember, don't you, Pastor, a couple of months later? Mary's father cashed in an insurance policy so Mary could fly to Denver and be with her new husband for just one weekend. It didn't make any difference that Tom would be out of the Air Force and back home in just a few more weeks."

"An insurance policy for three days ..." mused the pastor.

"Your father had a judgment about the impracticality of that, didn't he, my dear?"

The pastor, indeed, still remembered the incident. In fact, each time she remembered it, she also remembered the catch in her heart the memory evoked.

"Well, Pastor," the Wise Old Woman went on, "the story of Mary and Tom is a little like this story of Mary and Jesus. There are times in life when practicality is set aside, when the cost of things isn't even a factor in deciding a course of action. This time in Jesus' life was one of those times. Mary, Martha, and Lazarus are aware of the threat to Jesus' life. They know he may be killed soon. If he is killed, these three are aware that Jesus' death is, in part, on their behalf. Mary is aware of the immensity of the kind of love Jesus has for her. She responds in kind. She anoints Jesus, filling the house with the fragrance."

The pastor wasn't paying too much attention to the Wise Old Woman's interpretation because she was thinking about the practicality of her life — the hundreds of times over the years she had counted the cost rather than simply loved. The pastor was once again aware of a feeling she had sometimes. She'd heard other people have it, too. It was a feeling edged with fear. Fear that she had missed something very important in life.

She interrupted the Wise Old Woman's sermon to ask, "What are those times, Wise Old Woman? What are some of the times when cost isn't even considered?"

"Oh," the Wise Old Woman answered, "They are once-in-a-lifetime times. I really can't be more specific because these times differ for everyone, depending on *their* lives. But, it might be a wedding, or maybe the celebration of an anniversary. It could also be something quite spontaneous, like spending your last $300 for a balloon ride or throwing dollar bills out a tenth-story window at a ticker tape parade. It could even be as foolish as cashing in an insurance policy for an airline ticket to Denver."

The pastor, intrigued, but not yet converted, wanted to argue, but the Wise Old Woman kept preaching.

"Though the circumstances may differ, there is one condition which is always the same about these times of impracticality. They are all times when love is so full — so overflowing — that one doesn't even think about counting the cost. The only thing that counts is the love and the wild, outpouring expression of it.

"It has been said there is nothing else in life as impractical as a love relationship," the Wise Old Woman continued. "This story about Jesus and Mary illustrates that statement. It has nothing to do with charity for the poor, my dear Pastor. That's another issue entirely. This story is simply about one of those times in which love is expressed without considering the cost.

"So," said the Wise Old Woman, turning toward the pastor, "have you ever experienced any of those times?"

The pastor wished the Wise Old Woman hadn't asked that question. She only remembered long years of counting pennies and never celebrating. The pastor further speculated that if she couldn't expend herself financially, did it mean she couldn't expend herself emotionally and physically and spiritually as well? Jesus had spent everything he had in a heart burst on the cross.

The pastor wasn't able to reflect further on her recollections because at that moment the Wise Old Woman began zipping up her neon suit, preparing to leave. The pastor suddenly realized if she were to have a sermon on Sunday, she'd better get some of the Wise Old Woman's wisdom.

"Wait a minute!" she said to her bright friend. "If the point of this sermon isn't about deciding where one spends one's money, what *is* the point?"

"I thought it was obvious, Pastor. Mary — Jesus' Mary — is so moved by his love for her that she simply can do nothing else but love him back as completely as she can. Mary's loving is a very sensual love. Not only does she pour a year's worth of wages over his feet, she wipes his feet with her hair. Jewish women never let their hair down anyplace but in their own bedroom. This is a very intimate scene. It seems to me that one point of the story is once we get ahold of how deeply we're loved by God, we simply can't do anything else but love back in the same way. Sensually, intimately, completely, without counting the cost."

"Does that mean expending everything and anything?" asked the pastor. "Money, reputation, even my life?"

"You know," continued the Wise Old Woman rather critically, "you Christians are all the time talking about God loving you and about receiving God's lavish blessings. Do you ever think about loving God or creation lavishly in return? That's what is happening in this story. Jesus accepts this abundant generosity which Mary literally pours over him.

"Do you ever think about how you also can love others in extravagant ways?"

The pastor was thinking about such a love relationship as Jesus and Mary. She was wondering if she would ever love so much that she would pour out a whole year's wages without thinking about the cost.

As if reading her mind yet one more time, the Wise Old Woman said gently, "I repeat. Nothing else in life is as impractical as a love relationship. And yet, such impractical expressions of love are never wasted. Mary's action is a response of joy!

"In the gospel writer Mark's account of this story, Jesus adds, 'The deed this woman has done is so great that wherever the gospel is preached, this story will be told and it'll be told in memory of her.'

"So tell the story this Sunday, my dear," said the Wise Old Woman, pushing back her chair and standing. "Tell it in such a way that Mary and all others who pour out love without counting the cost will be remembered."

Realizing her friend was about to leave, the pastor quickly reached for pencil and paper.

"Remember Mary? Which Mary?" the pastor asked. And when she looked up for an answer the Wise Old Woman was gone. The pastor began to write, hoping she could remember just half of what the Wise Old Woman said should be preached for the coming Sunday morning.

# The Wise Old Woman's Thanksgiving

## Luke 17:11-19

*It was a* once-upon-a-time in a small northern Wisconsin town. Full-page grocery ads for turkeys, blaze-orange hunting suits hanging across porch railings, and snow spitting against her cheeks as she walked to the post office let one of the pastors in this town know it was close to Thanksgiving. Normally, this pastor would be happy. She considered herself a thankful person. But on this particular once-upon-a-time the pastor was distressed. She was responsible for a sermon on Thanksgiving Eve. She was supposed to inspire folks to feel thankful, to experience grateful hearts. The worst was happening. The pastor was not feeling thankful.

"It's an occupational deficiency," moaned the pastor to herself. "How can I inspire grateful hearts, or any other kind of hearts, if I'm not feeling grateful?"

With the first bunch of Indian corn in early November, the pastor had begun checking the temperature of her soul. She checked and rechecked. As the November days went by, she continued to come up with the same coldness.

Tired from work with budgets, letters about finances, planning for Advent and Christmas, the pastor tried to whomp up some thanksgiving. She tried singing "Count Your Blessings." She read scripture. Psalms were good. She looked for stories of others who were grateful. She recalled times in her own life when she had been filled with gratitude. But trying to create a thankful heart only heightened her deadness, and thus, added to her despair.

31

The pastor finally had to face the fact she had exhausted her own resources. It was time to consult the Wise Old Woman.

The pastor had confidence in her strange friend. Even though the Wise Old Woman dressed funny, she was a good listener. Encounters with the Wise Old Woman were always helpful.

The pastor didn't know much about the Wise Old Woman's personal habits nor how to contact her, but she knew the Wise Old Woman often hung out in a restaurant, and she seemed to like French Town Custard best. So, on the Monday before the Wednesday Thanksgiving Service, the pastor headed for French Town.

Imagine her surprise and relief when she spotted the Wise Old Woman in her usual spot in the back corner of the restaurant.

"The signs are good!" thought the pastor. "She is alone and she has on the purple sweatshirt. I am sure to get something from the Wise Old Woman. I am sure to gain some insight for Wednesday night." The pastor hurried toward the back corner.

"Hello, my dear," said the Wise Old Woman. She seemed genuinely pleased to see the pastor. "I didn't think I'd see you for a few weeks. Busy time of year, isn't it? I didn't think you'd take any time to relax, to enjoy these last fall days."

Somewhat embarrassed by the Wise Old Woman's chiding, the pastor wondered briefly if her workaholism had anything to do with being tired, and, thus, not thankful.

"Well, actually I am not here to relax," she responded. "I came looking for you, Wise Old Woman. I need help again."

The Wise Old Woman, of course, knew of the pastor's plight all along. That is why she is called the Wise Old Woman, after all, and why she gets to wear those letters on her sweatshirt. She was also a Compassionate Old Woman (never mind the acronym denoted with this appellation!), and she took the pastor's dilemma seriously.

"How can I help?" she said.

"Oh, Wise Old Woman. I have to preach a Thanksgiving sermon this Wednesday and I'm not feeling thankful. I'm supposed to be a spiritual leader. I'm supposed to model faith, provide a vision, and be authentic while doing it."

"I get the picture," the Wise Old Woman interrupted. "You're supposed to be some kind of spiritual cheerleader?"

The pastor had heard the phrase, but was reluctant to apply it to her behavior. She projected. It was the Wise Old Woman who looked like a cheerleader, with a purple sweater with school letters dancing across her chest.

The Wise Old Woman interrupted the pastor's thoughts again, this time with understanding.

"It must be a bad spot. I suppose you've tried the old blessing count." The pastor nodded. "And scripture?" the Wise Old Woman continued. "Psalms?"

"Yup," said the pastor, hoping the Wise Old Woman wouldn't start asking about all the stuff she'd read.

Instead the Wise Old Woman asked, "What scripture are you using on Wednesday night?"

The pastor, prepared for just such a question, reached for her briefcase and her Bible. "Well, I brought the scripture along. Let me read it to you. Jesus and his disciples are heading for Jerusalem. Here's what happens."

> On the way to Jerusalem Jesus was going through the region between Samaria and Galilee. As he entered a village, ten lepers approached him. Keeping their distance, they called out, saying, "Jesus, Master, have mercy on us!" When he saw them, he said to them, "Go and show yourselves to the priests." And as they went, they were made clean. Then one of them, when he saw that he was healed, turned back, praising God with a loud voice. He prostrated himself at Jesus' feet and thanked him. And he was a Samaritan. Then Jesus asked, "Were not ten made clean? But the other nine, where are they? Was none of them found to return and give praise to God except this foreigner?" Then he said to him, "Get up and go on your way; your faith has made you well."

As the pastor came to the end of the scripture reading, she barely took a breath before commenting. "The story is simple, Wise Old Woman. There are ten lepers. They ask Jesus for mercy. When

Jesus tells them to go show themselves to the priests, it means they are already healed. Lepers who had been cleansed were required to be pronounced clean by a priest before they could officially resume their place in society. In heading for the priests, the lepers indicate they believe they're already healed. And, they are. All ten of them! However, only one comes back and thanks Jesus. The twist (there's always a twist) is that the one who comes back is the Samaritan. Though they shared ancestors in the faith, for generations Jews and Samaritans hadn't shared Torah interpretations. Even *healthy* Samaritans are outcasts, according to Jews. The implication in the story is the other nine lepers are Jews. Jews are supposed to be closer to God, their rituals enacted from a grateful heart. Jesus is confronting people of his own faith. He's calling them to question the condition of their own hearts. These Leper-Jews are obviously not grateful.

"Just like me, Wise Old Woman. I claim to be a Christian. I want to live out all my life in a response of thanksgiving for God's saving grace through Christ. And, here it is Thanksgiving, and I'm not thankful! This scripture makes me feel worse, like a leper. I feel guilty, hollow, like an unstuffed turkey."

The pastor sighed and leaned back in her chair. The Wise Old Woman saw her chance at last and quickly broke the silence.

"Let's take the focus off *you* for a minute, my dear. Let's look carefully at what happened in the story. The lepers meet Jesus. They ask for mercy. Jesus says, 'Go to the priests.' This means the lepers are already cured; cured, it seems, by simply asking for mercy and then believing mercy has been given to them."

The pastor noded at the Wise Old Woman's observation.

"Who will be at this Thanksgiving service, pastor?" The Wise Old Woman really didn't want the pastor to go off on another diatribe, because she quickly answered her own question. "I'll tell you who will be there. There will be some folks who are tired and some who are thinking about a half-done Jell-O salad in their refrigerator. There will be folks who are struggling with disease and some who have fallen short of their life's goals. There will be some people who think they are too fat, too thin, too old, too young. Some of the people gathered will be fighting with their relatives.

Others will be folks who have done something they know is bad and the memory and secret of it cripples them. There may even be folks like you, who wish of all times of the year they could feel thankful at Thanksgiving.

"All those folks," continued the Wise Old Woman, "may think for one reason or another *they* are lepers. Isolated outcasts. Ones who are desperately in need of God's mercy.

"Notice what happened to the lepers, my dear. They meet Jesus, ask for mercy, and *believe* him when he indicates they already have it! Did you notice that their perception of their health changed *before* they even looked down at their skin to check on their condition for themselves?

"All you need to do Wednesday evening, my dear, is remind people gathered that through their baptism they have already met the crucified and risen Christ, they already have God's mercy, and they only have to act as if they believe it to experience a thankful heart."

Then, remembering another part of the story, the Wise Old Woman mused, "I guess the point of the story is not the miracle of healing, but the attitude one takes when one discovers the gift of God's grace."

The pastor, however, wasn't listening. She was trying to let a feeling of God's mercy sink into her. How wonderful even in her ungratefulness to again feel God's mercy.

The Wise Old Woman didn't seem to notice the pastor's pensiveness. Seeming to warm up to her subject, she began to sound like a preacher herself. A Preaching Old Woman. Here, in front of the pastor, she was winding up for the P.O.W. POW!

"For heaven's sake, Pastor, whoever said *you* had to *feel* thankful in order for others to feel it? That's your ego at work, inflated to the highest degree. Remember Luke's story? God gives the healing. God is in charge of the change of heart as well. You say you feel like a leper? Do you believe mercy has already been given to you? Why not act as if you believe it! If you want *my* advice, you'll relax a bit. Quit trying so hard to do the work only God can do. Order a cup of coffee and just sit here in the sunshine and visit with me awhile. Laugh a little."

The Wise Old Woman's invitation was tempting. The coffee smelled good. So, that is just what the pastor did. And, miracle of miracles, as she drove away from French Town Custard, the pastor felt a strange, but vaguely familiar feeling in her insides. Could it be? She whipped out her soul thermometer. Yes. Yes, it was ... a glimmer ... a glittering, actually. It was much like when morning sun shines through a restaurant window and finds rhinestones on a sweatshirt. It was a fair shimmering of thanksgiving! The pastor felt grateful for all sorts of things, but particularly for friends such as the Wise Old Woman. Turning the corner onto Washington Street and seeing the church, the pastor broke into the first stanza of "Come, Ye Thankful People, Come."

She hurried into her office and flipped on the lights and the electric typewriter. "Now," she thought. "Now is the time to get ready for Wednesday night."

# The Wise Old Woman Says Good-bye

## Matthew 9:35—10:8

*A thunderclap awakened* the Wise Old Woman with a snap. She peered out at the June morning with sleepy eyes. It was Tuesday up above where the thumb of Wisconsin sticks out like a hitchhiker into Lake Michigan. She had *heard* — the way Wise Old Women hear things — that the pastor of that two-point charge was moving south the next day and she had not yet said, "Good-bye."

The Wise Old Woman wondered if the pastor would look her up before she left. And, somewhat vainly (only a little vainly because any woman who makes it to old and wise has very little vanity left), the Wise Old Woman wondered if the pastor would thank her for the help she had given her. The Wise Old Woman was always there when the pastor needed her.

"Well," thought the Wise Old Woman, "we usually meet in a restaurant. I think this morning I'll go over to Hardee's — have a cinnamon raisin biscuit and twenty-cent coffee."

Wise Old Women know things others don't, of course. Sure enough, the pastor's car was in Hardee's parking lot and there was the pastor sitting in the corner, amidst a Bible, tray, papers, and coffee. She was writing furiously.

The pastor noticed the Wise Old Woman immediately. She couldn't miss her, really. Outlandish clothing ... make-up. Today, the Wise Old Woman had on her familiar purple rhinestone initialed sweatshirt. (The letters W.O.W. often lit up at special moments of insight for the pastor.)

"Oh, Wise Old Woman, I'm so glad to see you. I didn't know how to find you. I never know when I'll see you ..." There was a brief realization on the pastor's part that the Wise Old Woman always seemed to show up at just the right time.

This time, of course, it was the Wise Old Woman who was looking for the pastor. She wanted to give the pastor an opportunity to say "good-bye." The Wise Old Woman wondered if the pastor would thank her. But the Wise Old Woman was polite as well as wise. It wasn't time yet for good-byes, so she referred instead to the pastor's activity.

"Are you working on your sermon already?"

"Yes. This is my last sermon here. I'm moving tomorrow. Did you know?"

The Wise Old Woman nodded, but she responded to distress which was written across the pastor's face.

"Well, Pastor, it's not unusual for you to have trouble with sermons. This one must be especially tough. Good-byes are hard."

"Yes," agreed the pastor. "I've been saying good-bye to individuals, but *this* good-bye will be in a sermon. I need to witness a good-bye in the context of the Christian community."

The Wise Old Woman wrinkled her brow. "I don't know what you mean ..."

"Well," explained the pastor. "It's sad to say good-bye. I have a lot of love and affection for the people I've been with. But every sermon is in the context of God's love. Good News. There's something more to say besides my sadness and good-bye.

"Frederic Buechner has a comment about doing sermons. He says something like: 'A pastor need tell only two stories: her own and God's. And, then tell how they intersect.' ... The quote is something like that. I can't remember exactly and I've packed the quote. *My* story is sadness at leaving beloved Christian friends. God's story? I'm not sure."

"Don't you usually have a scripture to work with?" asked the Wise Old Woman, getting into her helping mode. "What do you call it — a pericope?"

(The Wise Old Woman was feeling another little piece of vanity at remembering a seminary word. Pericope ... sounded like the little tube of mirrors which sticks up out of the water from a sub-marine and looks around for enemy ships.)

The pastor, though a bit surprised at the Wise Old Woman's vocabulary, began describing the pericope: "Well, Jesus has been proclaiming and sharing God's love ... healing and teaching around Galilee. He probably realizes he needs help. There are lots of powerless folks who need teaching and healing. Matthew calls them 'sheep without a shepherd.' I hate that term. But I learned that in Greek it simply means 'grassroots people' (no pun intended). They were common people. Some Jewish religious leaders held the common people in contempt because they didn't have the money or the education to obey the religious laws. Jesus has compassion for and wants to reach the common people.

"There are LOTS of common folks. And, in this text, Jesus chooses help. Matthew gives us their names. Jesus gives them authority to heal and preach God's love and sends them out to do it.

"I'm stuck, Wise Old Woman, because this story — GOD'S STORY — seems to be the beginning of a ministry, not the end-ing. My story as pastor in Abrams and Oconto is ending. Matthew's text which calls the disciples is 'Hello.' The situation on Sunday is 'Good-bye.' "

The Wise Old Woman realized immediately the connection of the pastor's story and God's story, but like a good Wise Old Woman she didn't tell the pastor. Rather, she began to try to help the pastor see the connection for herself. She asked, "Pastor, what cap-tures your interest the most in this story?"

"Oh ... the NAMES. Jesus called specific people with specific names. Just like all of us at baptism. We're called and included in Christ's Body (God's family) by our names. We're KNOWN. I'll be saying good-bye to specific people — called by name. Names I learned, people I love. We were sent out to serve God together for five years. We've proclaimed God's love, healed and learned together ..."

The pastor's voice trailed off and she began to softly name the disciples she knew: "Melvin, the fisherman ... Vernon, son of Wil-liam ... Pearl, the Abrams-ite ... Al, the one called Peanuts ... Kim, the teacher ... Gary, father of Brian, Bill, and Scott ..."

The Wise Old Woman wanted to interrupt, but she knew how important it was that the pastor remember each of those people she loved and was leaving. She remained quiet like a good Wise Old Woman. Several minutes went by. And then the pastor blurted, "Oh, Wise Old Woman ... in preparing this sermon, I read in the commentaries that by the time Matthew wrote this, the early church had already forgotten the names of the first disciples. Matthew named them as a reminder, I suppose. Wise Old Woman, will that happen to me? Will I forget the names of my brothers and sisters in Christ? Will they forget me?"

"Now," thought the Wise Old Woman, "is the time to speak."

"Perhaps, my dear," she said tenderly, "you'll forget and they will forget you. We all forget events and names and important things even when we are reminded by daily contact. If the early church forgot the names of the FIRST disciples ..."

The Wise Old Woman decided not to finish the sentence although she was tempted to point out the pastor's vanity a bit and help the *pastor* become a bit wiser. But, instead, she continued, "They may forget you. You may forget names ... but you will remember your ministry together."

The pastor nodded, and the Wise Old Woman asked, "What WILL you remember?"

"Oh, I'll remember little events. The firsts. My first baptism ... wedding ... funeral. I'll remember Edna's egg carton angels, Chunky's 'sail deer,' Kathy's flowers, Shirley's Father's Day sermon, Bernard's coffee.

"But most of all, I'll remember growing in my faith because the people accepted me as their pastor. And I'll remember it's here I finally saw God's spirit at work in the church between people — between disciples. I had doubted, you know. I had been in the church for over 45 years and wasn't sure the church still listened to God or acted as if God's love was to be proclaimed. But I have seen God's Spirit at work here and have heard God's love proclaimed. I have seen teaching and healing and sharing. I am so grateful to the people of God in this place."

"So what is it you think God wants said, my dear? What is God's story for this Sunday?"

"I think God wants me to say 'Thank you.' Then I think God wants me to remind folks of their name — their sacred calling. The 'Hello to Christ' in their lives. I think God wants each one reminded that their baptism has given them power to heal and share Good News. God wants folks to hear again they are SENT. God wants me to acknowledge we'll say 'good-bye' and we'll be in different places, AND we'll keep on doing God's work together."

And, with those words the Wise Old Woman knew the pastor had made the connection between her story and God's. She listened as the pastor wrapped it up.

"Yes, I see. God is sending me out. And, God is sending the people, too. Into new relationships with each other. Into a relationship with a new pastor, who is also experiencing hello and good-bye with people. This Sunday is 'hello and good-bye and hello' all folded together."

The Wise Old Woman waited expectantly. There was only one item of unfinished business on her agenda with the pastor; the good-bye between *them*.

It was as if the pastor had read the Wise Old Woman's mind. With great affection she looked straight into the eyes of her friend and said, "Wise Old Woman, I want to say 'thank you' and 'good-bye' to you, too.

"I don't know how to thank you. You can't know how much you've helped me, not just with sermons, but with my *life*. How will I ever get along without you?"

"I don't ever leave you, my dear. You're moving to Kenosha? You'll find me there somewhere. Or, I'll find you. You'll probably be in a restaurant, fussing over your sermon. Maybe you'll be in 'Frank's Diner' or 'Simpson's' and you'll notice a funny-looking old woman. Maybe she'll have on a black turban with snapping eyes to match. Maybe her voice will sound like crackling thunder. And, you'll know ... you'll recognize ...

"You know. You remember the periscope — excuse me — the pericope? There's ministry to do and God sticks with God's people to uplift and uphold and sustain and love as the work is being done."

Stunned by the possibility of the Wise Old Woman's continued presence in her life and also stunned by her uncanny knowledge

41

(How DID she know about Frank's Diner and Simpson's?), the pastor didn't notice the Wise Old Woman stand up, straighten her sparkling shirt, and head for the door of Hardee's. It wasn't until she saw the strange figure hurry past the window, her skirt billowing in the wind and rain, that the pastor whispered, "Good-bye. Shalom."

# The Wise Old Woman Walks On Water

## Matthew 14:22-33

*Once upon an August* morning, the pastor of a two-point charge in the southeast corner of the state whose thumb sticks out into Lake Michigan like a hitchhiker rolled over, stretched, and worried herself out of bed. Though the morning was warm and didn't have a cloud in the sky, there was a big cloud in the mind of the pastor. She was distressed because it was Thursday and the sermon for Sunday wasn't done. It wasn't even started.

Adding to her distress was the fact the pastor had recently moved to these parishes. She still felt new. Though she was making new friends, she missed some of her old ones. Especially, she missed the Wise Old Woman.

The Wise Old Woman is indescribable as a friend and as a woman. She wears strange clothing, gaudy jewelry, and wild make-up. Most often the Wise Old Woman wears a purple sweatshirt with her initials in rhinestones across the front. The pastor counted on the Wise Old Woman for help with her sermons. In conversation, at the very moment the pastor received insight, the Wise Old Woman's initials seemed to light up in a glittering WOW! Here it was Thursday. The pastor needed the Wise Old Woman, but she did not know how to contact her. She didn't know where she lived and didn't have a telephone number. Furthermore, even though the Wise Old Woman seemed to run into the pastor just when the pastor needed her, she always did the running into in the northern part of the state. The pastor had moved 200 miles south and on this beautiful summer morning was sure there was no hope of seeing her old friend.

The pastor stopped at the post office, drove to one church office to answer phone messages, and then headed toward the other church office. She realized she had better prepare *something* for Sunday.

While driving south on County Trunk MB, the pastor noticed an old woman walking into Bristol Woods County Park. The figure looked familiar. Could it be? It certainly looked like the Wise Old Woman. The pastor got excited. Yes, there was the purple sweatshirt. There was only one sweatshirt she knew with initials W.O.W. The old woman turned and the sunlight sparkling on the rhinestones revealed WOW! It was the Wise Old Woman! She was here!

The pastor pulled over and jumped out of her car. "Wise Old Woman! Is that you? Really you? What are you doing here? Are you visiting someone? On vacation? How did you get here? I don't see a car. Did someone drop you off? Do you need a ride? Were you expecting to see me?"

The Wise Old Woman, used to such an attack of questions from the pastor, who was a rather excitable personality, simply smiled and waited for her to stop talking. Then she answered, "I'm just out for a walk. It's such a beautiful morning, not a cloud in the sky. This park is such a pleasant stop. Rolling hills. Green. I can smell the corn growing. Pastor, I was just going over to sit under that huge oak. Will you join me?"

The pastor, still not quite believing her friend was here, fell into step alongside her. She decided it would be impolite to immediately ask the Wise Old Woman for help with her sermon. Social amenities dictated she would have to wait a bit.

The women walked up a knoll to a picnic table under the oak tree. They swung their legs over the bench and were quiet for several moments, enjoying the morning sounds. A dog barked in the distance. Locusts hummed. A soft breeze whispered through oak leaves.

The Wise Old Woman finally broke the silence.

"So how are things going, my dear?"

Relieved to be talking, the pastor's words spilled out all at once. "Basically very good, Wise Old Woman! I've had a lot of changes since I saw you last. I got married. I changed my name. Moved. Started to serve God in this new place. I'm doing a lot of adjusting. But, things are going very well," the pastor paused, "... except ..."

"Except for your sermon on Sunday," finished the Wise Old Woman, once again indicating either her wisdom or intuition. "You're having trouble with your sermon," she continued, "which seems to be a common problem with you."

The pastor nodded her agreement.

"Well, as long as I'm here, we might as well talk. What is the problem?" asked the Wise Old Woman.

The pastor explained, "I'm usually stuck on some part of the scripture, or I'm stuck on just what to say out of several possibilities, but this time it's the text *itself*. It's the story of Jesus walking on water. I'm frustrated. I'm not sure what I believe about it. I have so many questions. How did he do it? *Did* he do it, or is it just a story the early church used for some reason? If so, why did the early church tell it and how did they use it? Should we tell it and use it, too? How? Are we supposed to believe Peter could walk on water and, therefore, as disciples we can, too?"

The pastor gasped for a quick breath and continued to pour out her distress. "The scholars aren't any help. They have trouble with the text, too. Some of them discount it. Some insist the event happened just as reported. Some say it was told to help folks through persecution of the church. Even though they don't seem to have a definitive answer, they put the story in a category. It's a Miracle Story, they say, and then they put it in a subcategory ... Nature Miracle."

The Wise Old Woman interrupted. "What do *you* think, my dear?"

"I really believe scripture is supposed to point to God and to raise questions for us to explore. I don't think definite answers are always possible. The most important question this text raises for me is: What does this story have to teach followers of Christ about their relationship with God?

"My friend, Hazelyn, says scripture is the meeting place between humans and God. We meet God as we hear and explore God's Word. In this story, Peter and Jesus *meet* on troubled water. Does that mean I'll meet God on troubled water? Does it mean I'm supposed to get out of whatever boat I'm in and be saved? The story seems to say in meeting God, fear gets in the way. It seems to say when we're in trouble we don't have to add to our woes by being afraid. God loves us and will save us."

The pastor took another deep breath and stopped.

Used to her verbosity, the Wise Old Woman savored the pastor's silence for a moment and then responded, "I think you've discovered a metaphor which speaks to you. Can you be more specific?"

"No, Wise Old Woman, I can't. At least I can't clarify my idea in a thesis statement. I do have images spinning around in my head."

"Oh? And what are they?"

"One is from the video *Romero*. Initially, Archbishop Oscar Romero identified himself with political leadership of El Salvador. Then, as he ministered, he saw the hardship of his countryfolk, oppressed because of corruption and persecution by the same governmental leaders. Even though frightened, Romero literally chose to walk on troubled water with the oppressed. He was shot and killed while giving communion.

"Romero is a well-known martyr, Wise Old Woman, but there are common people who are heroes and saints, too. I know people who do little acts of courage. They are folks who, even though afraid, take small steps one at a time on troubled water.

"Like Sherry. Her husband was killed last spring in an industrial accident. She has three children to raise and knows she can't do it without further schooling. She is scared to death to go back to school, but three weeks ago she signed up for a fall course. She knows God is calling her in the midst of her trouble. She's stepping out of the boat.

"And, there is Neal. He's gay. He feels a strong call to come out of his boat of fear and tell his father about his lifestyle. He loves his dad and doesn't want to hurt him and make a worse storm. He's taking steps to tell, even though he knows he may sink.

"I wish you knew Bob. He was trained to be an architect, but has always had a dream to produce low-cost, flexible modules for homes. Such modules could be easily constructed and then dismantled and even moved. Bob just turned 45 years old and realized if he doesn't act soon, he may never realize his dream. He is afraid, but he quit his job, found a small apartment, and set up his workroom. His family and friends are critical, but Bob feels called. He has just finished his first experimental jig.

"Do you understand, Wise Old Woman? These folks all have fear, but their faith lends them courage to step out and walk on water anyway."

"And you, my dear?" asked the Wise Old Woman.

"Of course. I have lots of fears. My first Sunday in these churches I had a knot in my stomach and a dry mouth. I pushed myself out of a big overstuffed throne, stood at the pulpit, and froze. I thought I was sixteen again at the Solo Festival in front of the judge, convinced I would forget the words to my song, and then I did! Suddenly, at the pulpit, the vast chasm of fear which I know I carry yawned and swallowed me whole. I know I can topple into those jaws at any minute. I have. But, I also remember God's saving presence is with me in the bottom of that pit, too. I inherited such grace through my baptism. I am loved and supported by a strength far stronger than spasms of fear.

"So, on that first Sunday morning, and lots of other mornings, I just took a deep breath and stepped out of the boat. So far, a saving presence has always snatched me to safety."

"Hmmmm," hmmmed the Wise Old Woman. "Is that why you're having trouble with your sermon? You're just afraid and haven't trusted God's spirit? If the scripture is a story, why don't you tell a story? A walking on water story. The early church told it as a story. Jesus told stories. Why don't you just tell a story?"

"A story?" The pastor expressed her horror. "What kind of a sermon is *that*? These folks don't know me yet. They'll think I'm nuts. It's bad enough talking to someone who for all I know is a figment of my imagination, a story in herself!"

The Wise Old Woman didn't even bat an eye at the suggestion she might not exist. She confronted the pastor right where she needed confronting. "It's *fear*, my dear. You're afraid of the opinions of your new brothers and sisters in Christ. Do you remember another scripture? Perfect love casts out fear!

"What's a sermon supposed to be anyway? Twenty-two minutes long? A thesis and three points? 'Long and boring?' as one of your new parishioners described?

"You should have acted on your impulse and purchased those huge plastic 'walking on water' boots you saw at Hammacher Schlemmer yesterday in Chicago. You could have taken the congregations down to Lake Michigan and had a demonstration sermon!"

Stunned by the Wise Old Woman's words, the pastor wanted to ask questions of her own. How did the Wise Old Woman know what her parishioners said about sermons? How did she know the pastor had shopped in Chicago the day before and laughed and laughed when she saw those huge yellow inflatable boots which looked like pontoons and sported an ad which claimed the boots allowed the wearer to walk on water.

The pastor thought her most creative solution would be to invite the Wise Old Woman to preach on Sunday, but the pastor knew better than either to invite her friend to preach or to ask her all those questions. She never received satisfactory answers from the strange old lady.

So instead, the pastor began to consider the Wise Old Woman's advice, a question the Wise Old Woman was at that very moment repeating. "Why don't you just tell a story on Sunday, my dear? A walking on water story? I thought a sermon was supposed to point to God's love. I didn't think there were any rules about how it should happen."

As the pastor began to consider the question, a ray of sun found a path through softly moving oak leaves and flashed on the rhinestone-studded sweatshirt. WOW! Wise Old Woman. W.O.W. Walking on Water. WOW!

The pastor laughed! She laughed not only at the sense of humor God must certainly have, but also at the wonderful, awe-filled power of God's love. She quickly fumbled in her purse to find some paper and pen. She wanted to jot down some notes for a story sermon. When she looked up, the Wise Old Woman was gone.

# The Touch Of The Wise Old Woman

## Mark 5:21-43

*Once upon a late* June morning in the southeastern part of the state with a thumb which looks like it's hitchhiking across Lake Michigan, a hot pastor, on her way to the office, stopped at Taste of Wisconsin for coffee and a muffin. The hostess greeted her like a friend, knew she didn't need a menu, and led her to her favorite table by the window, which had already been set up for her by the waitress who saw her coming.

"How nice it is to be known," thought the pastor as she thanked the two women and sat down. She had been a pastor in the area for a whole year now. She was no longer new. How nice it was to know people by their names. How nice it was to know some family connections, even though she knew she would never get all the relationships figured out. And, how nice it was to be able to reflect on her parishioners' day-to-day lives. How nice it was to respond directly to their needs as she prepared for Sunday mornings.

Sunday mornings, of course, were a regular focus of this pastor's week. God's word needed to be proclaimed, both for the people and for God. Indeed, the pastor's mind, even as she sipped coffee and swallowed muffin, was on the upcoming sermon. With sudden awareness, the pastor realized it had been almost a year since she had seen her friend, the Wise Old Woman.

The pastor most often bumped into the Wise Old Woman when she needed help, especially help with the sermon. But on this hot June morning the pastor was simply lonely for her old friend. She wasn't really stuck with the sermon.

The scripture for Sunday was a familiar story, a story within a story. There was a spate of scholarly material to help her. However, it would be so good to discuss the text with the Wise Old Woman. She challenged the pastor. More than that, the Wise Old Woman had some kind of magic, a special power. The way she walked, the way she gestured with her hands, the way her strange clothes became like curtains which separated to display mysteries of the universe, all awakened the pastor's wonder. The presence of the Wise Old Woman was always a WOW! for the pastor.

As the waitress refilled her coffee cup, three loud, fiftyish businessmen were being shown to the very next table. "The rest of this room is empty," noticed the pastor with irritation. "Why are these men seated smack-dab next to me?" Her frustration didn't have a chance to take root, however, because as she was pinching the last crumbs of blueberry muffin from her plate, a strange yet familiar figure sauntered into the room and came directly to her table.

"Well, hello, Pastor. I thought I might find you here."

Excited and grateful at the same time, the pastor looked up and grinned. As if in answer to a prayer or a wish, the Wise Old Woman stood before her. Instead of the purple rhinestone-studded sweatshirt, the Wise Old Woman was dressed rather conventionally. A soft, blue dress, about the color of her eyes, hung in gentle folds over an undefined shape. The pastor would not have recognized her friend had it not been for her voice and her eyes, which were a deep blue-violet, like windows to the Wise Old Woman's soul of gold. Another surprise for the pastor was the appearance of a child, a girl about twelve years old with a thin, sad look. The child, almost hidden behind the Wise Old Woman, looked quite hungry. She was dressed in clothes way too big for her body.

"This is Joanne," said the Wise Old Woman. "Joanne, this is a special friend of mine." Introductions complete, the Wise Old Woman pulled back a chair for Joanne and seated herself with acquiescence, as if she knew she was there by invitation and for a definite purpose.

While glad to see the Wise Old Woman, the pastor had lots of questions. She had questions about the sermon, to be sure, but she was also curious about the child. Thinking it impolite to ask and not wanting to embarrass either of her guests, the pastor simply said, "I'm glad to see you, Wise Old Woman. I'm somewhat ashamed because I haven't kept in touch with you like I promised."

The Wise Old Woman seemed to ignore the pastor's apology. She gave her attention first to the child and then the waitress. She ordered a large breakfast for each of them and then responded to the pastor.

"I see your pen and paper, my dear. You're working on your sermon?"

"Well, not exactly *working*. I've done my reading and research. I'm kind of waiting for what Fred Craddock calls an 'Aha Moment.' You probably won't believe this, but I've been thinking for the past couple of days how good it would be to discuss this scripture with you."

"Oh," said the Wise Old Woman, feigning some interest. "Why?"

"I guess it's because one of the characters is a suffering woman. She's been bleeding for twelve years. She's not only experiencing physical suffering. She suffers emotionally and socially as well. She's been an outcast all those years. Untouchable. Separated by religious laws from her husband, family, and friends. I'm sure she's been trying all sorts of cures. I think I like her because she has guts enough to slip through crowds, which would be hostile to her presence, and touch some fringe on Jesus' tunic. I admire her courage."

"Oh," said the Wise Old Woman. "Isn't that scripture from Mark a story within a story? Isn't there a sick child, too? A child as old as the woman's illness? A child of an important Jewish leader?"

The pastor nodded, making a brief connection with twelve-year-old Joanne, the twelve-year-old daughter of a synagogue leader, and twelve-year-old hemorrhaging.

"Yes, Wise Old Woman, that's the story."

"Well, what have you learned from all your study?"

"Lots of interesting stuff, some of the information just recently discovered. There is fascinating detail about Jesus' clothing, a tassel in particular which would have been on his tunic or outer robe or sash. Even more interesting is a single blue-violet thread within the tassel. That thread would have been very valuable. The blue dye used for its color came from the tip of a certain snail. A hole was drilled through the shell, the dye extracted. It took 12,000 snails for a thimble full of dye. A pound of silk dyed that color cost $12,000. Of course, a pound of silk material would have provided a tiny piece of thread for everyone in the country. All Jews, at least male Jews, had to wear it. This piece of royal blue-violet thread symbolized social status, authority, and purity."

"My, oh my, Pastor, you *do* get down to details, don't you?" clucked the Wise Old Woman. "How do you ever get all of it said? Your sermons must go on forever, like boring lectures!"

The pastor appreciated the candor of her friend and was accustomed to the Wise Old Woman's affectionate chiding. At the same time the pastor became alert and expectant. From experience, she knew the Wise Old Woman would soon begin to ask the *important* questions, questions which would help the pastor get to the heart of God's word revealed through this story.

As if reading the pastor's mind, the Wise Old Woman continued, "Although the information on snails and twelves and tassels is very interesting, it is not where your attention lies, is it?"

"No," the pastor admitted. "The information *is* interesting and folks may like to hear it, but ..." The pastor left the end of her sentence unfinished.

"Where is your interest, my dear?"

"It's in the moment of the touch itself, Wise Old Woman. The instant the suffering woman's finger touches the tassel, she is healed. She can *feel* it!

"I keep visualizing the scene. The woman, sneaking up behind Jesus, is probably bending over, covering her face with a shawl. She wouldn't want to be recognized and driven away by an angry crowd. Most suffering people I know, myself included, become wiped out with long suffering. We become withdrawn, hopeless, and depressed. But this woman has energy and courage to reach out. It's just a touch and she's whole again."

"Not quite," cautioned the Wise Old Woman. "There's more."

The pastor thought carefully. "Well, Jesus feels the exchange of some kind of energy. He asks who touched him."

"Yes?"

"Well," continued the pastor, her curiosity aroused, "the woman, though she's full of fear and trembling, tells the truth. She exposes herself. She touches Jesus again. This time it is with words. Jesus tells her that her faith had made her well."

Satisfied she had heard the entire exchange, the Wise Old Woman waited, wisely, for the pastor's next wondering.

"Wise Old Woman, while I'm drawn to that touch, the physical connection between Jesus and the woman, I still get confused and frustrated."

"Why, Pastor?"

"The power of God is intense, beyond my understanding. I'm attracted to it and afraid of it at the same time. When Moses came near the burning bush, he knew he was on sacred ground and whipped his shoes off. Remember the man in Second Samuel who tried to help keep the Ark of the Covenant from falling? He touched it and was struck dead! The apostle Paul was knocked to the ground and blinded by the same power this hemorrhaging woman encountered. God's power is frightening and God's touch makes us whole. Or dead. The contradiction seems absurd, especially when our hunger for wholeness is so strong.

"Doesn't everyone long for God's touch? We want to be whole."

The pastor continued, "I think of television evangelists telling us to put our hands on the television screen, a safe enough point of touch, I suppose. I once received a letter from Oral Roberts with a piece of cloth which was supposed to be a piece of his shirt. The touch of God's power would be transmitted to me whenever I touched that scrap of material. If I donated to Oral Roberts' cause, I imagine I would feel more honest about receiving the power. While I laughed at the square inch of shirt, I don't laugh at my ache for God's touch. I think people I serve are hungry for healing and wholeness, too. Some of us need healing for our bodies. Some of us need healing from the horrors in our minds. Some of us need healing in our relationships. Some of us desperately want healing for others we love. But, what can I do, Wise Old Woman? I proclaim God's power is already with us through our baptism into Christ's Body, but we don't control that power, fascinating and frightening though it is. I'd like to wave a magic wand or lay my hands on someone and have all their suffering wiped out."

"Me, too, my dear," the Wise Old Woman replied pensively. She had been listening carefully to the pastor's monologue. For a moment her attention wandered to the quiet child to her left, eagerly chewing her food. Then she continued addressing the pastor.

"Perhaps Jesus didn't control God's power either. Healing for the bleeding woman, indeed, most healings, seem to require a connecting between the person and God. Before the connection, the person has to be in touch enough with his or her hunger for God to *reach out*, to have courage to act on one's own behalf. Perhaps a prayer evoked by this story is for our hunger for wholeness to be stronger than our fear of God's power."

The pastor thought about the hemorrhaging woman, how when she reached for Jesus, in spite of all that was against her, she demonstrated such courageous desire for God's touch. God responded.

The pastor noticed the Wise Old Woman and the child had finished their breakfast. She remembered all the other questions she had. Who was this child? Why did the Wise Old Woman have her along? Was there a significant connection between twelve-year-old Joanne, a twelve-year-old daughter of a synagogue leader, and a twelve-year-old illness? Did this child represent the rest of Mark's story?

The pastor, ready now to talk with the child, was dismayed to see the Wise Old Woman and the child pushing themselves out of their chairs.

Of even more distress was the realization she hadn't formulated a single question or heard a single answer in the conversation which would unwrap the scripture and reshape it into a sermon for Sunday.

As the Wise Old Woman and child turned to leave, an anxious pastor asked, "So, in this exchange between Jesus and the suffering woman, are you saying God's power is in touch asked for and given within the Body of Christ?"

With rising fear and a bit too desperate the Wise Old Woman would leave without giving her an answer, the pastor reached out and touched the blue-violet sleeve.

"What should I say on Sunday, Wise Old Woman?"

Either the words from the Wise Old Woman or the touch of her garment (the pastor wasn't sure which) sent a tingling energy through her body.

The Wise Old Woman took the pastor's hand in her own and smiled. "As Jesus says, 'Your faith makes you whole.' You are a good pastor, my dear. I'm sure you'll think of something."

# The Wise Old Woman Goes Fishing

## Luke 5:1-11

*In the once-upon-a-time* world and the real world, it was finally winter. The pastor of a two-point charge in the southeast part of the state whose thumb sticks into Lake Michigan like a hitchhiker sat at Taste Of Wisconsin peering over a cup of coffee. She watched through the window as county trucks sprayed wide circles of salt on a highway where the wind had swirled slippery spirals of snow. The pastor was preparing to go on a three-week break from her work. She wanted everything in good order and under complete control before she left, which meant the bulletin and sermon for February ninth had yet to be prepared.

As often happens, the pastor was stumped by how to preach the scripture story for Sunday. She wasn't hindered by lack of information or lessons deduced from the story. Her dilemma was that this particular story and its lessons were so familiar. She had heard Luke's story of the disciples' fishing trip and its many interpretations several times before. The story seemed stale, lifeless.

"I sure could use the help of the Wise Old Woman," thought the pastor, and then she quickly looked around the restaurant because every time she called her, it seemed the Wise Old Woman showed up!

The pastor grinned as she thought of her friend — such a strange apparition, one whose flashy jewelry and silvery hair would add instant sparkle to a gray day. The pastor sat thinking to herself, "Once upon a time a pastor sat watching winter. Hmmm, I'm in a story, too, like the story from Luke. *Anything* can happen in a story!" The pastor was just thinking those words, and sure enough, anything *did* happen! The Wise Old Woman, brushing snow off her sleeves and looking slightly more rumpled than usual, ambled into the dining room. She was dressed in the familiar purple sweatshirt with her initials W.O.W. in rhinestones across the front. The shirt behaved like a neon sign shouting WOW! whenever sunlight or even inspiration hit those letters.

The Wise Old Woman trudged straight over to the pastor's table. "Good morning, Pastor."

The pastor was glad to see her friend and was especially appreciative of the warmth of her greeting on this below zero wind chill factor day.

"How *are* you?"

The pastor had been asked that question a lot lately. Visions of doctors, medications, needles, tests, waiting rooms, and bills briefly flickered like a fire in her mind, but she simply answered, "Fine, thank you!"

The Wise Old Woman, who didn't get her name from nothing, observed wisely, "I know your body hurts, my dear. As your friend Rusty says, 'Nothing's right when your underwear's tight.' I suppose your spirit hurts, too. Therefore, I surmise you are stuck with your sermon."

The pastor loved these encounters with the Wise Old Woman. She could be honest with her questions. Indeed, the Wise Old Woman honored questions as if the questions themselves were sacred. The Wise Old Woman always asked more questions than she gave answers. Yet, somewhere in the conversation with her, answers seemed to bubble up within the pastor as if there was a deep well within and answers had lain submerged in life-giving water all along.

Lost in thoughts of sermon and well and water, the pastor suddenly remembered Luke's lake.

"Yes! Yes, Wise Old Woman. I could use some sermon help. The text is from the Gospel of Luke. It is his account of the miraculous catch of fish."

"Uh huh," the Wise Old Woman nodded, as if she also knew the story and its fine points inside out as well.

"The truth is," continued the pastor, "I'm sick of it. Maybe I'm not sick of the story," she hastened to qualify, "as much as what has been said about the story."

The Wise Old Woman thought, "No wonder she's blocked. She doesn't want to muddy the waters with more words." To the pastor, however, she said, "What *has* already been said, my dear?"

"Scholars compare Luke with other Gospel accounts," began the pastor. "They point out that in Mark and Matthew, the disciple Andrew is named, and in John the number of fish is set at exactly 153.

"Then they discuss which title for Christ should be used: Master, Teacher, or Lord? Then they argue if the word for boat is singular or plural. They wonder why Luke writes Lake Gennesaret instead of the Sea of Galilee. They argue whether the story took place before or after the resurrection. They discuss its genre. Some insist it is a nature miracle and, having a name for it, seem to dismiss it.

"That's only the scholars. The preachers aren't much better, Wise Old Woman. Some try to explain the miracle. For instance, one preacher claims Jesus simply stood up in the boat and he could see where the fish were! Some preachers spend their sermon time in a travelogue: they paint the picture of Galilee, the mountains, the lake, the ruins at Capernaum, the fisherman and fishing techniques of first century B.C.E. Worst of all, in my mind, are the preachers who stretch Jesus' metaphor too far. They take fisherpeople literally. I already have trouble with the image of shepherd, which seems to relegate disciples to dumb, bleating sheep. But *fish*? We know what happens to caught fish! They either end up over the fireplace on a varnished oak board, or end up slit, gutted, scaled, cooked, and placed on a *smorgas*bord."

The pastor's soliloquy had frozen her further into long-time winter. She sat silently, her body shivering into cracks. She didn't say the words aloud, but she realized every week she arrived at this point in her sermon preparation, the point of *her* limitations. She knew scripture is not to impart information. Scripture is to help bring about transformation within those who encounter it. God is in charge of the transformation department, the pastor only too painfully admitted. She could only point to a mystery which wouldn't even stand still.

The Wise Old Woman interrupted the preacher's despair. "Well, what part of the story captures your interest, my dear?"

(At this point in this once-upon-a-time story, it must be noted the Wise Old Woman refrained from a whole *string* of fish puns. She chose not to say, "*Reely*, Pastor, for no *porpoise*, whatsoever, other than the *halibut*, I'm *perch*ed here *floundering*, until I *sea* what *hooks* you.")

The pastor, completely unaware of what could have been the *fin*ish of serious conversation, was clear in her response to the Wise Old Woman's question.

"Oh, Wise Old Woman, I'm mostly caught by Peter's transformation! Peter leaves everything. He is abruptly changed by what he has seen."

The Wise Old Woman pursued, "What does Peter's transformation mean for your life, or the lives of people who will gather to worship on February ninth?"

"Peter's experience," responded the pastor with assertiveness, "is an epiphany, an encounter with God. Epiphany means made manifest. Peter sees God made manifest. Luke's story includes characteristics of all epiphanies. Through a burning bush, or an angel, or a fiery pillar, or Jesus, God appears and in the presence of the divine, the human is aware of his or her unworthiness. Do you remember, Wise Old Woman, that Peter said, 'I am a sinful man'? Then God, in this case manifest in Jesus, comforts and encourages and makes a promise which is also an invitation."

The pastor paused, reflected, and then continued, "I know encounters with God are dangerous; there is always change. That's why my attention is on Peter. I want to be changed, too. I think folks who gather on Sunday mornings want to be changed. I imagine they each have something in their life they want transformed.

"But, we are also different than Peter. This is Peter's first call. For Christians, baptism is the number one Epiphany. Through water and words of grace, God touches us and our lives are transformed.

Most of us are called before we are even conscious of it. We only grow into awareness if we stick with the Body of Christ. I'm sure each of us has epiphanies. If we recognize them, we usually can't explain them."

"Have you had such experiences, Pastor?"

"Yes, and they sound like the biggest fish stories ever. Oh, Wise Old Woman, why are we so hesitant to talk about miracles in our lives?" The pastor became quiet. She remembered epiphanies in her past: an earring glistening in February mud, a descant to "Whispering Hope," a dream symbol, a dot of ink no bigger than a mustard seed she carried on purple paper in her wallet.

The Wise Old Woman prodded the pastor from her reverie. "You said you identify with Peter. How?"

"Right now I identify with Peter just *before* Jesus showed up. He's finished a long night's work, an unsuccessful, long night's work. Peter is tired, probably dejected. Before he can rest, however, he needs to wash the nets and mend them if necessary.

"I'm tired. I want rest, but before that can happen, I need to have my tools in order. I need to get a sermon done, a bulletin. I need to make phone calls, and so on.

"I'm not unique. Most people can easily identify with hard work, some of it unsuccessful. Folks tell me about their need for rest and other tasks they need to do first.

"In addition to our livelihoods, we baptized folks have ministry to do. I suppose you could call our work fishing expeditions," the pastor laughed. "It's tricky for Christians to try to do God's work because God is in charge of miracles. Transformations occur within our hearts. Success in ministry, some people would say 'net results,' is hard to see. The success belongs to God, too."

The Wise Old Woman nodded and commented, "You noticed God showed up and the miracle happened when Peter gave up for awhile. Do you just need to give up working for awhile, lose control?"

The Wise Old Woman's question caused anxiety within the pastor. She had been raised with the Protestant work ethic as a primary value. She had spent much of her life believing her worth was based on her productivity. The pastor often didn't feel worthy unless she was fishing like crazy. However, she *did* want to change, and so she considered the Wise Old Woman's question carefully, and, after some silence, said, "Perhaps if I stop and look, I'll see God's presence again, made manifest in the midst of my brothers and sisters in Christ. Perhaps, like Peter, I'll experience another epiphany."

"Like NOW," thought the Wise Old Woman, but she didn't utter a sound. Rather, she twisted around in her chair, hoping the ceiling lights would hit the initials on her sweatshirt and reflect inspiration to the pastor. When her action didn't seem to elicit the hoped-for response, she said, "Pastor, have you heard the story of the desperate little fish who swam all over looking for the ocean?"

The pastor shook her head "no."

"That's the story, my dear," chided the Wise Old Woman.

The pastor looked confused, then caught on. She smiled, and briefly remembered Jesus, God on earth, pointed to God's Realm by telling stories. For a moment, although there was no sunshine, an unusual light flickered around the Wise Old Woman and danced off the rhinestone WOW!

The pastor was about to comment, but the Wise Old Woman was standing, ready to leave.

"Sounds like you already have your sermon, Pastor. And, tell people not to feel *gill*ty about taking a break. It gives one a chance to see miracles." And with that, the Wise Old Woman was gone.

# The Wise Old Woman Watch

## Luke 12:32-40; Jeremiah 18:1-11

"**You're stuck again**, aren't you, my dear?"

The pastor of the two-point charge in the southeast part of the state whose thumb sticks up like a hitchhiker going across Lake Michigan was shocked. She hadn't had time to arrive at the once-upon-a-summer-Friday-morning-time and here was the Wise Old Woman leaning against the outside doorway of Nikki's Restaurant.

The pastor, used to seeing the Wise Old Woman in clothing which announced her presence like a fanfare, was surprised to see her friend in a lumpy shirt and wrinkled blouse. The Wise Old Woman looked as if she'd just grabbed the apparel from the bottom of a sale table at Wal-Mart.

No matter what she wore, the Wise Old Woman always seemed to be available whenever the pastor was having trouble formulating or articulating a sermon. In fact, the pastor had awakened early on this very Friday, anxious. The sermon for Sunday was not even begun.

"I need to be rescued," the pastor thought as she had cleaned her glasses, just a few minutes before driving toward Nikki's. "I need the Wise Old Woman. I wonder where she is."

Now, here she *was* at Nikki's front door, acting as if she had nothing else to do but wait for the pastor.

The pastor's first words to her friend were words of admission, relief, and amazement, all at the same time. "Yes, I'm stuck. It is good to see you, Wise Old Woman."

Tears formed around the edges of the pastor's eyes. "It's been awhile since I've seen you. Will you join me for breakfast and conversation?"

"Of course," answered the Wise Old Woman, acting as if the whole scene had been foreordained.

The two women entered the restaurant, sat at the pastor's favorite table by the window, and ordered coffee and bagels from Joanne, the waitress.

"I have the same problem I usually have," confessed the pastor. "I get excited by the scripture and my study. It's fun for me and I want to share *everything*, but then all the information and ideas floating around in my head get jammed up, kind of like hermeneutical constipation."

The Wise Old Woman blanched a bit at the pastor's blunt description, but she was polite as well as wise and didn't comment. Rather, she responded, "I have all the time you need, my dear. Tell me what excites you about the scripture for this Sunday."

"First there is the story itself," said the pastor, getting right into her description. "It is Luke's account of a scene in a wedding. Wedding customs in Jesus' time were very different than ours. The celebration couldn't begin until wedding negotiations were over."

"Negotiations?" The Wise Old Woman seemed puzzled. She was thinking about the thousands of decisions modern-day brides and grooms are forced to make: whom to invite, colors of bridesmaids' dresses, how to light the unity candle, what to do with Dad's present wife, etc., etc.

"Yes." The pastor was eager to elucidate. "The groom negotiated terms of the marriage with the bride's family. They were economic terms. The bride price. I suppose it might be jewels or money, cows or goats. Whatever. The terms of the bargain might be argued for hours and even days, and the deal could be struck any time of the day or night. The groom's friends, family, and servants, if he had them, waited with the horns, hats, confetti, rice, bird seed, ice cream, and cake. They were waiting for the negotiations to end and the celebration to begin. They wanted to be at the party, alert and awake!"

The pastor summarized, "That is the first set of stuff floating around in my head. The second is information about how the early church used this gospel story. Scholars agree the story was used to teach Christians *watchfulness* and *fidelity*. They were waiting for Christ's second coming and they believed it would be any day. They were reminded they needed to be faithful and devoted to their duty. One duty was to *watch*.

"Here's one of the major differences between Christians now and then," continued the pastor in her teaching mode. "Now, it is 2,000 years later. What about Christ's second coming? Christians have had lots of time to discuss and argue questions like, '*When* will the second coming occur?' and '*How* will it happen?' and 'Is it here already?'

"We have had 2,000 years to come up with big words and bigger definitions, like realized eschatology and future eschatology."

The Wise Old Woman wrinkled her nose. "You lost me, Pastor."

The pastor straightened her pedagogical hat. "It is natural for humans to speculate about end times. Eschatology means a discussion about last things. We have stories for beginnings. It is natural to have stories about our endings. There is an amazing variety of ideas and big words about eschatology: annihilationism, apocalyptic literature, apocatastasis, chiliasm, demythologization, hell, Kingdom of God, limbo, millenialism, parousia, resurrection of the dead ..."

The Wise Old Woman put her hands up in front of her face as if to ward off further attack. "I'm interested in what *you* believe, Pastor."

The pastor surprised herself with a ready answer. "I mostly try to live in the now — realized eschatology. I believe God's Realm is already here. Jesus continually said, 'The Kingdom of God is in your midst.' However, I also realize, no pun intended, God's reign is not yet complete. So, I buy the Christian understanding of living 'in between times,' in between the now and the not yet."

The Wise Old Woman looked stunned, as if the pastor had launched into speaking in tongues. The pastor, seeing her friend's eyes glaze over, spoke louder, trying to explain.

"We rehearse this belief in our sacrament of communion. In the Great Thanksgiving we say, 'Christ has died; Christ is risen; Christ will come again.' We live in between times. I know it is confusing and gets some of us nuts."

The pastor stopped talking. She was beginning to notice the *now* that she was in. The Wise Old Woman was silently and deliberately dividing her pat of butter into equal fourths and very carefully putting each piece on a quarter of her lightly toasted bagel.

"Pastor, I know you." The Wise Old Woman was pensive. "Even with your 'blockage of ideas' (the Wise Old Woman had more 'couth' than the pastor), I know you have a question rolling around in your brain with all that other stuff. What is your question, the question this scripture from Luke evokes?"

The pastor took a deep breath and relaxed into her chair. The Wise Old Woman was demonstrating why she was such a dear friend. She knew the pastor through and through and made space for her. The Wise Old Woman's careful listening and pointed questioning led the pastor to discover what was already within her, present but unseen. She responded gratefully, "Yes, I do have a question. If one lesson for the church from this scripture is to watch faithfully, my question is: 'What am I watching *for*?' One question for people, gathered on Sunday as the church, is: 'What are *we* looking for?' If we are to train and encourage each other to be faithful in watching, don't we have to train ourselves to be looking for something specific?"

The pastor barely stopped for air before continuing, "My question brings me to another topic which has been swirling around in my head: the comparison of Bible times and our times when it comes to watching. People in Jesus' time had to rely on people watches: wedding party, soldiers, shepherds, guards at the gate. They needed to hone their senses of sight, sound, and smell. We rely more on electronic devices: computers, electric eyes, burglar alarms, smoke detectors, radar, weather balloons, Rolexes which beep on the hour. The people waiting for a groom in our time could turn on a motion detector, which would set off an alarm, turn on lights, get the CD going, and activate robots to throw confetti and have ice cream ready all as the groom is turning the corner a block away. They could be sleeping and still be ready!"

A little too animated, the pastor continued, "In addition, there is a question I have about motivation. Watching for the groom is only a metaphor. The early church was watching for Christ. They were doing it because they didn't want to miss the party. They wanted to be included in God's Realm. They talked about the messianic banquet, another Jewish end-time story, in which everyone is invited to a heavenly feast."

Afraid the pastor was getting carried away, the Wise Old Woman interrupted. "Do you remember your first question evoked by this scripture, my dear? What are *you* looking for?"

"I think I'm really looking for a party." The pastor seemed uncomfortable with her answer. "Often, when I enter a church function and people are milling around, I hear myself say, 'Oh, is *this* where the party is?' People laugh sometimes and then the milling goes on. I haven't seriously considered that a party is exactly what I want. I know I want God's presence with me. I want to be included in God's Realm, which I believe is already here. I wonder, Wise Old Woman, do you think other people want a heavenly banquet now, too?"

Not giving her wise friend a chance to reply, the pastor added, "The Hebrew scripture for Sunday, from Jeremiah, sounds like a threat. Jeremiah's words could be interpreted, 'Be faithful in your watching or else God will get you!' Maybe we've misinterpreted Jeremiah. I believe when God has us, which is already the case, it's *good*. Good News.

"Like now. Look out the window, Wise Old Woman. It's a beautiful August morning, the beginning of a day. In a few hours, some of us will participate in an end-time story. I'll lead a service of death and resurrection for Esther. Earlier this week I participated in a beginning-time story. Trevor Allyn Matson reached up, pulled off my glasses, peered directly into my eyes, *watched* me carefully as I baptized him. The day marked his first birthday and his birthday into the Body of Christ. Realized eschatology, beginning and end, life and death in this world all wrapped up."

The pastor again *realized* the *now* she was in. "There's Joanne. She's pushing three tables together and setting up places for ten women. 'There is a once-a-month-party,' Joanne said." The pastor pointed to a half glass of water in front of her. "I wonder if at their party, this lemon slice water tastes like wine?"

The Wise Old Woman and pastor were quiet for a moment, each reflecting on the mystery of life unfolding before their eyes.

And then the Wise Old Woman reached in her purse and pulled out a tiny box of pink. They were matches from the Queen's Table Dining Room at the Santa Maria Motel in Key West, Florida. Telephone number: 305/296-5678.

Less anxious now, and therefore able to be more watchful, the pastor *watched* as the Wise Old Woman struck one of the matches and lit the tiny hurricane lamp filled with green liquid to match Nikki's placemats. And if the Wise Old Woman had worn her purple sweatshirt with her initials across the front, it would have been precisely at that moment the rhinestones would have reflected the light and glowed WOW!

No longer fretting about finishing a sermon, the pastor *realized* she was at that very moment at a party. She turned her attention to watching faithfully and further *realized* she was now ready to begin writing Sunday's sermon.

# The Wise Old Woman Intrudes

## Genesis 9:8-17; Mark 1:9-15

*It was Fat Tuesday*, the day before Ash Wednesday and the beginning of Lent. The pastor of a two-point charge in a rural township in the southeastern corner of the state whose thumb sticks out into Lake Michigan like a hitchhiker was driving down Highway 50 into the sunset.

She was on her way to the Bristol Town Hall for the unveiling of a new town logo.

Things were going well with the pastor. It had been a beautiful day, the temperature in the 40s. It had also been a productive day. The Ash Wednesday supper and service were pretty much in shape. Sunday's bulletin was done. Plans were going well for the Bolivian Festival. She'd made phone calls and hospital calls and even had time for thirty minutes on the exercise bike.

Now, she wondered who would be at the unveiling. As faces of town residents flicked through her mind, the internal video was interrupted by a troubling thought: "What if I run into the Wise Old Woman?"

Now the pastor dearly loved the Wise Old Woman. She was a friend she could count on, especially when she needed help with her sermon. But the pastor didn't need help this week, either with her sermon or anything else. In fact, the pastor hadn't needed or seen the Wise Old Woman in a long time. Folks at the churches she served were beginning to ask, "Hey! Have you seen the Wise Old Woman lately? What's happened to her?" The pastor briefly wondered if the folks were hinting her sermons needed help, but she quickly dismissed the thought.

As she reached the intersection north of town and turned left on 200th Avenue, the pastor was surprised to find herself hoping the Wise Old Woman would not be at the Town Hall. She appreciated the Wise Old Woman's help when she needed it, but she didn't need help now. In fact, the pastor was simply too busy this week to fit in a conversation with the Wise Old Woman. Conversations with her took time. They became deep and probing and required thought. Sometimes there were even long, long silences.

The pastor pushed down on the gas pedal. She was busy. Impatient. This was the first week in Lent. She didn't have time to talk. She needed to get things *done*!

She steered her car around construction equipment on 83rd Street, parked in the west lot, walked past two men in business suits, and entered the Town Hall. The atmosphere inside was festive, as if a party was going on. She saw a long buffet table full of food, a podium with lights and microphones. Next to the podium was an easel, mysteriously draped with a gray velvet cloth.

Bustling in between furnishings and other people were town residents familiar to her. Carol, Gloria, and Edith were carrying platters and cups. There was Merle, Audrey, and ... was that familiar form over in the corner of the room, hanging up her coat, the Wise Old Woman? Yes, it was. The pastor didn't recognize her at first because her friend looked rather plain. There was no garish clothing, no painted fingernails, no rhinestone monogram. The Wise Old Woman, on the contrary, looked tired, lonely, and *old*.

"I can't hide from her," the pastor thought, feeling a rush of affection. "She's helped me so many times."

The pastor couldn't have escaped her friend even if she'd tried. The Wise Old Woman put her coat on the rack, turned, and came directly across the room to the pastor, as if she had known the pastor would be at the event. The Wise Old Woman, indeed, seemed to be on a mission.

"Good evening, Pastor." There was a slight smile.

"Hello, Wise Old Woman." The pastor felt embarrassed and somewhat guilty. She launched into a string of excuses for not being in touch. "I've been so busy. You know what my schedule ..."

The Wise Old Woman interrupted the brief confession. "It's okay, my dear. I knew you would be here and I came to see you."

The pastor was puzzled. Wasn't the Wise Old Woman interested in the new town logo? And how did she know she'd be here? The Bristol Grapevine is incredibly efficient, but the only person the pastor told about her plans had been her husband.

The pastor averted the Wise Old Woman's penetrating gaze by eyeing little egg salad sandwiches, ham rolls, and a specially decorated cake, like the town logo still under wraps, on the table. The Wise Old Woman said she was always looking for a party. Wasn't that why she was here?

Waving an index finger to capture the pastor's attention, the Wise Old Woman persisted in conversation. "So tomorrow is Lent," she began. "How is everything going, Pastor?"

"Fine, just fine," replied the pastor, relieved at the question. She felt especially competent with the topic and with her list of completed tasks. Everything accomplished ahead of time. She began to tick off her deeds as if they were trophies, but the Wise Old Woman interrupted again.

"You have everything in perfect control, then?"

The pastor nodded. She was so pleased with herself. Smug, actually.

"How about your Sunday sermon?" pressed the Wise Old Woman.

Usually, the pastor initiated conversation about the sermon, and it was usually because she needed the Wise Old Woman's help. But not *this* week! With pride she answered, "Oh, the sermon is in great shape. I've got lots of ideas. Earlier today I went through my files. I have more than enough material, a surplus of illustrations."

The Wise Old Woman raised weary eyebrows. The pastor felt one of those long, long silences coming on. She anxiously and stupidly began talking to fill it up.

"The Gospel text for Sunday is Mark 1:9-15. Seven packed verses. Jesus is baptized and he's not even dry yet before he's off to the wilderness. He resists temptation by Satan and comes out again, knowing how and what to preach!

"The Hebrew scripture is about God's covenant with Noah. All through Lent the churches I serve are remembering the promise we have with God through our baptism. How we keep breaking our promise and yet are continually offered the possibility of new beginnings by God who keeps the covenant."

The Wise Old Woman nodded as if she was interested, and then asked, "What will you say on Sunday, Pastor?"

"Well, I'll tie the floodwaters to the waters of baptism. I'll talk about our covenant with God through Christ to fight sin and then I'll hit us all about how we keep breaking our promise and succumb to temptation. I'm going to elaborate on *sin*."

"Hmmm." The Wise Old Woman looked pensive. "I thought you preached Good News."

"Oh, well, yes ... but it's Lent. This is a time of self-examination. In our baptism we make a promise to follow Jesus, and then we break our promise. There are so many ways we break covenant, so many ways we hurt ourselves and others."

The Wise Old Woman noticed the pastor was warming up to the subject of temptation.

"You know, Wise Old Woman, there is a whole continuum of temptation. At one end there may be a simple enticement of chocolate to a person on a fat-free diet. At the other end there may be a crisis in which folks simply choose to quit believing in God's love and take their own life or the lives of others."

"I can tell you really like sin, Pastor! It's clearly a subject of which you're an expert."

The pastor didn't know how to take the Wise Old Woman's comment. As she was mulling over a response, she noticed town officials were ready to unveil the logo. The pastor sneaked a look at her watch. She needed to be home by 7:00 to receive a phone call. She really didn't want to pursue this conversation with the Wise Old Woman. She needed to head her off, and she also didn't know how to come right out and tell her she didn't need her. So the pastor said, "Thank you, Wise Old Woman. However, as I have already said, I have more illustrations and stories for Sunday's sermon than I can ever use."

The Wise Old Woman seemed amused. Rather than sink into her customary long silence, she began a barrage of questions.

"Aren't you the pastor who has been quoted as not knowing why we work so hard during Lent? Aren't you the one who goes around reminding folks that for almost 2,000 years the Easter story has turned out the same? That Jesus is always resurrected? That people don't have to do *anything*? That God does it *all*?"

"Well, yes." The pastor was taken aback.

The Wise Old Woman, however, was not finished.

"Don't you preach God's grace, that you can't do anything to receive new life? That God's continued covenant offer is a gift?"

"Yes ..."

The pastor remembered the Wise Old Woman wasn't called wise for nothing. She figured the Wise Old Woman had a point she was about to make. The pastor's anxiety increased. What was the Wise Old Woman really saying?

"And, Pastor, couldn't extra hard work and being in control and in charge of everything be succumbing to temptation, too?"

"Oh-oh," the pastor thought, beginning to feel like a trap was about to be sprung and she was the prey. She noticed the Wise Old Woman didn't look tired, lonely, or old anymore. In fact, fire seemed to be lighting up her eyes. The pastor froze as the Wise Old Woman came in for the kill.

"Pastor, doesn't all sin occur when folks think they don't need God? When they think they can do it *all* themselves?"

In that moment, everything crumbled within the pastor. She who had been so sure of words, illustrations, a continuum of ways we avoid God by doing what we think needs to be done even in God's name, wasn't so sure. Here was this old woman — her friend, to be sure, her life-giving friend — calling everything she had prepared into question.

It was too much. The day and the week which seemed to be going so well were now as unknown to the pastor as that logo under its gray veil.

She felt the Wise Old Woman's judgment. She resisted the guilt which rose from the soles of her feet. "Guilt isn't in these days," she said to herself silently and then was dismayed to hear herself say aloud in an angry, defensive voice, "Wise Old Woman, what are you asking of me? I can't preach perfect sermons. I can't get through worship without making some stupid mistake. I can't even say no to chocolate. None of us lives up to our own expectations of ourselves. Everyone I know is tempted away from God somehow. Why, Jesus *himself* had to be ministered to by angels. Even the Son of God couldn't have survived in the wilderness without the gift of God's grace."

Then came the long silence. Long silences, which are so hard to come by, are, at the same time, often fruitful in their offerings. And, in that particular long silence, the pastor heard her own words and made the connection. She realized she had succumbed to one of the worst temptations. She'd turned down God's help when she needed it most because she was certain she didn't need it.

All at once, several things happened. Edith and Carol uncovered the cake. The town chairman lifted the veil. Flashbulbs lit up logo and cake simultaneously and matching words of frosting and paint revealed "The Town of Bristol, Naturally."

Over the applause, the pastor whispered to the Wise Old Woman, "Did I say 'even Jesus needed help'?"

With a wide smile on her face and bright reflection in her crisp blue eyes, the Wise Old Woman turned and answered, "I'm glad you heard yourself, my dear. Yes, even Jesus couldn't fight temptation all by himself. He needed angels."

"You mean we need each other and God most when we think we don't?"

"Precisely," said the Wise Old Woman, and turning toward the cluster of activity around the new town logo, she added, "I think that will preach!"

With another flash of light she was gone.

# The Wise Old Woman On The Loose

## John 14:15-31

*Once upon an early* Friday morning in May, the pastor of a two-point charge in the southeastern corner of the state whose thumb stretches out into Lake Michigan like a hitchhiker woke up. Though at first confused with her surroundings, she remembered she was in the Best Western motel in Wisconsin Dells. She was with a group of clergywomen who had hired a consultant to teach them about power equity. The group had spent all day Thursday learning what happens with groups when members have equal access to power. They were experiencing what the consultant called "loose energy."

During some of yesterday's loose energy, the pastor bumped into her clergy sister, Joan. They caught up on news and then Joan said, "Do you ever see the Wise Old Woman?"

"My gosh!" said the pastor, "I'd forgotten all about her! I haven't seen her for awhile, not since the unveiling of the Town of Bristol's new logo. That was over a year ago."

"Well," said Joan, "I think she's here at this retreat. I saw her name on the list of registrants."

For the rest of the afternoon and evening the pastor was on the lookout for her old friend. She looked around the room and in the hallways carefully and even checked the pool and lobby areas, but she didn't spot the Wise Old Woman.

The pastor was used to having the Wise Old Woman show up almost anywhere, even in this saturated playground of Wisconsin, but here it was Friday morning and the pastor hadn't seen anyone resembling the Wise Old Woman.

"If she *is* here I'll be sure to spot her," the pastor assured herself. "The Wise Old Woman sticks out in a crowd." In fact, just the other day a parishoner asked, "Where's that friend of yours? That Weird Old Woman ... or is it the Wacko Old Woman?"

The pastor defended her friend. "God is often revealed in the unexpected," she preached. And weird, wacko, wily, or wise, interaction with the Wise Old Woman always included insight. The pastor deeply appreciated the "Ahas" accompanied with flashes of light which danced off the Wise Old Woman's rhinestone-initialed sweatshirt.

Now on this Friday morning, a very early Friday morning, the pastor rolled out of bed. It was 5:07 a.m. Could she find a quaint little coffee shop? An open quaint coffee shop? After driving down main street and back, she gave up, pulled into Country Kitchen's parking lot and was heading toward the door when she noticed a very familiar figure coming her way.

The two women greeted each other with genuine affection. "I was told you were in the area, Wise Old Woman," the pastor smiled. "Won't you join me for breakfast?"

"Of course," her friend replied, as if that was the whole reason for her being up and out at this ungodly hour in this ungodly place.

A hostess seated the women in a booth near a window. By looking carefully past cars, concrete, billboards, and neon signs, the women could see a tiny strip of river and trees, the natural beauty of the Dells all but blotted out by water slides and miniature golf courses.

They ordered, were served, and visited a bit over their food about the power equity retreat. They laughed about loose energy and then spoke more thoughtfully about the mysterious uplifting power which seemed to surround them.

As the waitress cleared the dishes, the Wise Old Woman said, "Well, Pastor, today's Friday. Your day off! Is your sermon done already?"

"No!" said the pastor a bit too loudly, indicating her stress. "I haven't even started it! Not that I have to preach a regular sermon every week, but somehow God's word of grace needs to be proclaimed every Sunday and I'm responsible to see the witness occurs and, this Sunday, as usual, the world of Jesus and our world seem to have irreconcilable differences. Completely disparate."

"What do you mean?" prodded the Wise Old Woman, knowing from experience the pastor tended to give long-winded answers.

"The scripture is from the Gospel of John. He is leading us through the Last Supper. Jesus is speaking to twelve men. Within 24 hours he'll be dead. That's the world of Jesus.

"In our world, it's May 14. Mother's Day. Our world will focus on women. Of course, the United Methodist Church prides itself on being inclusive, so we will celebrate the Festival of the Christian Home."

"Hmmm," said the Wise Old Woman. She was good at hmmmms and silences, which seemed interminable sometimes, but which allowed both reflection and deeper insight to occur.

The pastor interrupted the hmmm.

"Our worship services are meant to include everyone. Not all worshipers are mothers. The Good News of God's love is for everyone there. But, Wise Old Woman, all week long, I've noticed mothers.

"I saw a picture of O.J.'s mom, her long, thin, thoughtful face. She had to be pushed into the courtroom in a wheelchair.[1]

"And I saw pictures of some of the mothers of children blown up in the bombing of the Murrah Building.[2]

"And Wednesday, I was the last customer of a waitress who was finishing her first day on the job. She saw her husband coming to pick her up. He had their baby in his arms. She literally ran to the door to meet them. She could hardly wait to get her hands on her child.

"And I've been listening to my clergy sisters. One of the hardest issues they face is being pastor *and* being mom."

The pastor reached into her purse and pulled out a cartoon.

"And look at this, Wise Old Woman. It's from the *New Yorker*." The Wise Old Woman grinned at a picture of a card rack in a department store. An ad for "Mother's Day Cards" was placed at the top of the rack. On the shelves, categories of mothers were listed for easy selection: Biological. Working. Surrogate. Adoptive. Earth. Single. In-Law. Unwed. Unfit.

"There's such a variety of mothers," the pastor observed. "They can range from Susan Smith to Mother Teresa." She stopped long enough to take a breath which gave the Wise Old Woman a welcome chance to respond.

"Well, not everyone who comes to worship is a mother, but they've all had one. Or still have one." The Wise Old Woman, by her remark, proved once again she comes by her name honestly.

The pastor agreed. "I'm remembering my conversation this week with a 45-year-old woman. She's married and has a couple of boys. Everything is going well. She has her health, a good job. Yet, she talks about an emptiness in her life. A hunger. She's seeing a counselor. She said to me, 'I think I'm just looking for a mother — a *good* mother.'

"Wise Old Woman, I think everyone needs a good mother no matter how old one is."

The Wise Old Woman looked thoughtfully at the pastor and then said, "I hear about that longing a lot. I've heard it from all sorts of people: men and women, young and old."

The two women sat in complete silence listening to their own words which seemed to bounce around and echo in a dark emptiness, a deep well evoked by simply naming the aching need at the center of our being.

Finally, the Wise Old Woman broke the silence. "You've reminded me Sunday is Mother's Day, but you haven't said much about the scripture you'll be reading."

"Ah," replied the pastor. "It's the passage from the Gospel of John about the Last Supper. It's very interesting, Wise Old Woman. Jesus knows he's going to die. He is preparing his closest friends, and, in his good-byes, he sounds like a mother!

"He says, 'I will not leave you *orphaned*.' Then Jesus makes a promise to the disciples: 'I'll ask God to send you an Advocate,' he says, 'the Holy Spirit.' "

The pastor launched once again into her teaching mode. "The word 'advocate' is interesting. Versions of the Bible translate it variously: Helper, Guide, Counselor. Scholars call it the Paraclete, which is not a little aqua bird who serves as a household pet, but a name for Jesus' presence when Jesus is absent!"

The pastor, noticing a slight grin on the face of the Wise Old Woman, was encouraged and continued, "It's hard to understand, Wise Old Woman. All these centuries we've just used the term Holy Spirit, but the presence described sure sounds like a *good mother* to me!"

"Hmmm," hmmmmed the Wise Old Woman, "a presence which is on your side, which helps, guides, and counsels. Didn't Jesus also say whenever two or three gather in his name, he would be there somehow? In some form?"

"Yes," the pastor agreed with some hesitancy. She wondered what the Wise Old Woman was driving at.

"Like now?" smiled the Wise Old Woman.

"Well ... yes," and the pastor began considering the presence of the Advocate right there in the Country Kitchen. As she considered, she noticed a slight flickering of one of the rhinestones.

"Or the clergywomen's gathering?" prodded the Wise Old Woman.

"Yes." The pastor smiled because she was remembering the tingling power of loose energy which bounced around the room in the Best Western. Her attention was drawn, however, to more rhinestones coming to life. Initials on the purple sweatshirt were beginning to shiver and shimmer.

"Or like Sunday mornings?" teased the Wise Old Woman.

And suddenly the Friday morning sunlight hit the W.O.W. in a full flash! The restaurant danced with light and the moment of insight broke through!

"Aha!" said the pastor with a quiet reverence. "Sunday mornings. Oh yes. Sunday mornings. The Holy Spirit. The Power of God on the Loose! The Power of God, like a Good Mother, always present, advocating, helping. guiding, counseling. Love on the loose! Wow!"

In her mind's eye, the pastor saw the people gathered for worship. She saw them as individuals, each one with a name, a family, a history, and each one with a mother. She saw each one with a longing, an emptiness which could probably only be filled by God's

Spirit. She saw each one immersed in and surrounded by that power given to them in their baptism and especially known to them when they gather together in Jesus' name. The same Jesus they will hear about from the Gospel writer, John. Jesus, soon to be dead, and then alive again, and on the loose!

The pastor saw the sanctuary just filled with that loose energy. More than really seeing it, she could just feel it. She could feel the loving presence of the Holy Spirit, a friend, guide, helper. Always there.

The pastor sat silently, basking in the light of loose energy, when suddenly her reverie was interrupted by another question.

"Is there anything *else* you need, Honey?"

The pastor thought it was the Wise Old Woman referring to sermon help and began to respond. But the person standing before the pastor wasn't the Wise Old Woman. It was the waitress. The Wise Old Woman was nowhere to be seen.

"Hah," the pastor grinned. "What a crazy idea. God like a Good Mother. God like Loose Energy. Even God, like a Wise Old Woman."

As she paid her bill and left the restaurant, she realized that even though she still had nothing to say, she could hardly wait for Sunday morning.

---

1. O.J. Simpson, accused of murdering his ex-wife, Nicole Brown Simpson, and her friend, Ronald Goldman, on June 12, 1994, was acquitted after a lengthy court trial.

2. The Murrah Building is the federal building in Oklahoma City which was bombed on April 19, 1995, killing 167 people. Timothy McVeigh was convicted of the crime.

# The Wise Old Woman Straight

## Jeremiah 1:4-10; Luke 13:10-17

*Once upon a sultry* August morning, the pastor of the two-point charge in the southeastern corner of the state whose thumb sticks out into Lake Michigan like a hitchhiker sat frustrated and motionless at her typewriter.

It was Friday, her day off. Her week had been busy with several intrusions. She had appointments scheduled through the next day, Saturday, and she had nothing prepared for Sunday morning. Pressure had given her a headache.

The pastor knew she was in good company. Lots of people in the congregations she served wandered around these days overscheduled, tired, headachy, and sometimes even bent out of shape.

The pastor had done her reading and studying of two scriptures, one from Jeremiah and one from Luke. She knew the setting of Jeremiah, the chaotic times in which he lived, and that God's call to him did not include a clear task such as many of the other prophets had received. She noticed Jeremiah was unsuccessful in his resistance to God's summons.

The pastor also had explored the Gospel story, a story about Jesus getting into more trouble. On a Sabbath, he reached out to a crippled woman who had been bent-over for eighteen years. She straightened up, immediately healed. Jesus didn't get into trouble because he healed her. He got into trouble because he had given God's grace at the wrong time. There was a clear religious rule: No work on God's day. Jesus' behavior continued to be an affront to church officials.

Here it was, the pastor's Sabbath. She stared at the typewriter. Her fingers didn't move. She wished the keyboard were a Ouija Board. She wished she had a little magic triangle which would float over the keys and spell out a sermon.

"Perhaps it is time for the Wise Old Woman," thought the pastor. The Wise Old Woman always helped when Sunday morning plans were not complete.

With an inert typewriter, a pressing schedule, and a headache, the pastor definitely needed the Wise Old Woman. She was just wondering where she might find her on this steamy summer day when the front doorbell rang. You guessed it! When the pastor opened the door, there was her friend, leaning against the porch railing, overdressed for the heat in her purple sweatshirt, studded with rhinestone initials.

"You rang?" grinned the Wise Old Woman as the pastor welcomed her into the living room.

"No, *you* rang," quipped the pastor, once again amazed at the Wise Old Woman's uncanny ability to be everywhere at once, at least everywhere at once when the pastor needed her.

"You're stuck again, of course," said the Wise Old Woman in a no-nonsense manner. She headed to the couch, plopped into its cushions, and pushed up the sleeves of her sweatshirt.

"Let's get this over with quickly, Pastor. I wanted this day off. I have other plans for today. Your request for my assistance with your sermon is intruding."

"Oh, I'm sorry, Wise Old Woman." The pastor was genuinely sorry. As long as her friend was giving her time, she would get right to the point. She explained, "The Hebrew scripture for Sunday introduces the prophet, Jeremiah, as a young boy. We learn he is special before he is born. Jeremiah feels he has no choice but to obey God's call.

"In the Gospel story from Luke, Jesus, who is also special before he is born, helps straighten up a crippled woman. The healing gets him into deeper trouble, and ..."

The Wise Old Woman, in a hurry and knowing how the pastor tended to go on and on, interrupted. "Which story captures your attention the most, my dear?"

"I can't decide. I can picture Jeremiah as a young boy with good stuff to say, but no one listening because he's a teen. I can empathize with the bent-over woman, but the encounter she has with Jesus isn't really about her. The story illustrates how his actions continue to humiliate good religious folks."

"Bent-over woman, huh?" The Wise Old Woman glanced thoughtfully over at the mirror on the living room wall.

The pastor, noticing, realized her friend seemed more burdened this morning. She thought, "Maybe the Wise Old Woman's interest lies with the bent-over woman." Her hunch was affirmed with her friend's sudden question.

"What do you know about the bent-over woman?"

"Not much," answers the pastor. "Biblical scholars say the words of Luke's Gospel in Greek were more about being *bound* than being sick. So, it is not exactly a healing which is being talked about. It is more like a freeing, an unbinding, a loosening up. That is why Jesus talks about untying oxen and donkeys. Animals were tied up on the Sabbath to lessen the work. There was a rule: No work on God's day. But owners still untied their animals to allow them to get food and water. Jesus' point, I think, is the woman should be unbound, too, in order to receive God's food."

"The woman was bound, huh? Is there anyone in either of your congregations who is bound, bent over with burdens or sorrow?"

"Oh, yes! There is hardly anyone who *isn't* bound somehow." The pastor, in her mind's eye, was seeing faces of people she had encountered during the week: people around the table at the leadership development event, in the pews at Grandma Joyce's funeral, in the hospital room with Shirley and Kathryn. She saw people in the office, at TOPS, at the worship committee meeting and people at a study group discussing women's issues. She remembered the news: Hillary Clinton going to the international women's conference in China, a country which used to bind women's feet. She remembered the coverage of Harry Wu's release.[1] It isn't just women who are bound, she thought. Men also have things which cause their bodies, minds, and hearts to sag. Young people, young boys like Jeremiah, and children are also bound by convention, conflict, laws, and unkind comments.

The Wise Old Woman broke into the pastor's reflection.

"So, Pastor, you're very aware of bent-over situations?"

"Well, I'm aware the sanctuary is filled with folks like the bent-over woman who long for untying. Freeing. I'm also aware we're sometimes like the officials who are confused about what God's work really is and when to do it, and we're called like Jeremiah to be messengers of God's grace, and we're called like Jesus to be agents of it. We're all the parts and all the people in these stories!"

"It's no wonder Christian folks feel overburdened, over-scheduled, tired, and headachy," said the Wise Old Woman, looking a bit more like a Weary Old Woman. "No wonder they need a day off!"

"I know," breathed the pastor in a longing whisper, "a Sabbath, a day of rest."

"It's interesting to me that on your day off you're working!" teased the Wise Old Woman.

"Well, am I really working? Or, am I answering God's call?" answered the pastor. "And, is it one or the other? I'm trying to find words to proclaim God's grace. All of us Christian folks are called to be agents of God's grace. Through our baptism, we're given the power to unbind and it is a 24-hour-a-day job, seven days a week. So, are we bound or free? The older I get, the less I can figure it out."

"Have you figured out anything?" asked the Wise Old Woman, hopefully. She knew *her* job was to push the pastor along until there was a moment of insight.

"Not exactly, but there *is* an interesting twist to the story."

"Yes?"

"Luke describes the woman as bent-over." The pastor stands up and bends over at the waist. "Luke must want us to see her body position is important because he reiterates: 'she could not stand up straight.' In those days, standing up straight was the posture for praising God.

"So, she could not praise God! Whatever the reason for her bent-over condition, she could not give thanks to God. Whatever bound her also prevented her from expressing her gratefulness.

"I think of dark moods I have sometimes. I'm so *bent-over* I can't see the light. I can't see hope. Thanksgiving is the last thing on my mind. I don't even think of thanking God in such a mood.

"When Jesus speaks to the bent-over woman, she not only stands up straight, assuming the posture for praise, she begins to praise. She doesn't thank Jesus, she thanks *God*!"

The Wise Old Woman, being wise, didn't respond. She knew silence at this moment would beckon the pastor to the edge of insight.

"Oh, Wise Old Woman, the bent-over woman has at the same time a change of attitude and a change of body. There is a before and after with God's grace somewhere in the mix, and I wonder, when I'm in a blue funk and needing a change of attitude, how it actually happens?"

The pastor kept talking. "I'm thinking what people say to one another when they're bound up and bent-over with stress and pain. They say, 'Count your blessings!' I hate hearing those words when I'm out of shape. The comment seems like another binding to me. Yet, when I'm thankful, my spirits straighten up, too. Which comes first, Wise Old Woman, the straightening, or the attitude of gratitude?

"What I really wonder, Wise Old Woman, is, if I'm in a blue funk and remember to be thankful, will I straighten up? Will I appreciate my life the way it is given and feel joy and hope again?"

"I can't answer that, my dear," said the Wise Old Woman, demonstrating yet again why she was called wise, "but, it is certainly worth a try." Then she added, "Isn't that why folks gather on Sundays to worship? Aren't they there to give thanks, to discover joy and hope again? It seems to me one point of Luke's story is: God's love doesn't play merely by rules. There is no prescription. Rules do not regulate God, but it is clear God's grace is found in compassion and understanding.

"After eighteen years," the Wise Old Woman pointed out, "someone finally noticed the woman's bent-over condition. Someone offered her compassion and understanding. Maybe when one is in a blue funk or *bent-over*, one can't control God's love, but one can look for it. Maybe someone will care, will notice distress, will offer compassion and understanding, and suddenly there will be straightening and hope. Let's say, for instance, that someone is bent out of shape because they need help with a sermon ..."

And, at that moment, the sun broke through the window, bounced off the mirror, and hit the points of the rhinestones. The pastor got the points! There was a gentle shimmer in the living room and in the living souls of the two women.

"Thank you, Wise Old Woman," said the pastor, overwhelmed with gratitude for the compassion and understanding of her friend. "You were at my door even before I thought I needed you. You listened to my distress. You saw *me* bent out of shape with tasks and long lists of limited time. You gave up some of your day off, your Sabbath, for me."

"Ah well," teased the Wise Old Woman with affection, "didn't some Gospel writer named Luke try to help folks see God's grace doesn't work with a schedule?"

"Yes!" the pastor laughed, getting yet another point, "and you've given up enough time for me today! I'll say hello to the folks at Wesley Chapel and Bristol who have been asking about you. I haven't the foggiest idea about other words I'll say on Sunday morning, but at this very moment I feel unbound and thankful," and the pastor stood up straight and walked her friend to the door.

_____

1. Harry Wu is a human rights activist who was sentenced by the Chinese government to fifteen years in prison for espionage and then expelled from China to his home near San Francisco.

# A Choosy Wise Old Woman

## Deuteronomy 30:15-20; Matthew 5:21-26

*Once upon a mid-February* Saturday morning, the pastor of the two-point charge in the southeast corner of the state whose thumb sticks out into Lake Michigan like a hitchhiker sped down Highway 50 toward her office. It was one of those days which couldn't decide whether it wanted to cling to winter or jump ahead to spring. First, there was sun and blue sky, then, overcast and gray. First a warm breeze tickled, then a cold gust slapped.

The pastor, however, hardly noticed the indecisive weather, because she had some deciding to do herself. Reverend Joyce Alford, the pastor's District Superintendent, had been scheduled to be in worship the next day. The two women had planned a dialogue sermon using the lectionary texts from Deuteronomy and Matthew. In Deuteronomy, Moses is preaching, "Choose life." In Matthew, Jesus is proclaiming, "Life is found in relationships with God and God's people." In the sermon, the pastor planned to ask Joyce, "Where *is* life in the Southeast District, and how might God's people at Bristol and Wesley Chapel participate in it?" Reverend Alford had promised to respond to the question by identifying specific spots in the district where she saw ministry alive.

Yesterday, on her day off, the pastor learned Joyce had found a spot in a district parking lot which was still clinging to winter. She had fallen and messed up her knee. Reverend Alford would not be in worship.

Of all her tasks, the pastor felt especially responsible for bringing Good News to people gathered on Sunday mornings. She felt the need to interpret where life could be found, to say nothing about choosing it. The pastor not only felt responsible, she really *wanted* to bring Good News. She needed to hear it, too, and to be encouraged to keep choosing it.

At this late date, however, the pastor was left with indecision. What should she *do*? Should she pull out one of the other two "Choose Life" sermons she'd preached in the past? Should she pore through books, stories, and magazines on her bookshelves? Should she tell the folks what had happened and offer them some options for Good News Time?

At the office, the pastor spilled the bad news to Lois, the secretary, who immediately moved Reverend Alford's name in the bulletin from the sermon to the prayer list. Then, the pastor grabbed an unused tablet and new pen and headed for Taste Of Wisconsin. Maybe, just maybe, she could find the Wise Old Woman.

Even though she considered herself to be on a mission to find her friend, the pastor had to admit more often it was the Wise Old Woman who found the pastor.

As she approached the restaurant, the pastor noticed the parking lot was already full. Her heart sank. The Wise Old Woman didn't like crowds. What should she do? The pastor couldn't decide. Should she stop at Taste Of Wisconsin or should she go on to Cracker Barrel?

There were dozens of other choices: Frank's Diner, Perkins, Stars and Stripes. The Wise Old Woman could be at any of those places and more. The pastor drove around the parking lot trying to choose. As she approached the front of the restaurant, she spotted a parking place right at the door. She took the opportunity as a sign, pulled in, parked the car, and went inside.

She looked around quickly, didn't see her friend, and her indecisiveness continued. "Should I sit down and wait for a few minutes? Which table do I want? What do I want to eat? Do I want *anything* to eat? Should I have another cup of coffee? Regular or decaf?"

The waitress, arriving at her left elbow, seemed to be in a rush. The pastor took a deep breath, made all the decisions before her, should have been relieved by her proficiency, but only discovered she had more decisions: How long should I wait? What if the Wise Old Woman doesn't come? What will I do for Good News if I don't see the Wise Old Woman?

The pastor was just getting fidgety when a familiar figure appeared at the entrance to the dining room. The Wise Old Woman waved to the pastor and indicated to the hostess she would join her friend by the window.

"What a relief," the pastor thought, "I am so glad to see her." Even as the Wise Old Woman was walking toward her, the pastor realized she still had a bunch of choosing to do: Exactly what kind of help did she want from the Wise Old Woman? How could she get her thoughts together about the scripture? What words would best describe her dilemma? Did the Wise Old Woman have enough time to spare? Did the pastor have enough money with her to treat the Wise Old Woman to breakfast?

With all these choices bouncing around in the pastor's head, the Wise Old Woman arrived at the table and sat down. The pastor had long ago given up trying to figure out how the Wise Old Woman knew when she needed help. She was just grateful her friend always appeared. The Wise Old Woman's presence itself was rich and grace-filled.

"Hello, my dear," the Wise Old Woman's greeting was warm. She smiled at the waitress, ordered tea and an English muffin, then turned to the pastor. "So, you're in trouble again, and it's *late* in the week. Usually you are ready by this time!"

The pastor, wishing the Wise Old Woman hadn't reminded her, nodded her head and described her dilemma: her D.S. with a torn ligament, people gathering hungry for Good News from God, and the expectation the pastor felt to have just the right words to say.

The Wise Old Woman responded to the pastor's distress. "You certainly get yourself in a tizzy, don't you, my dear? How can I help?"

"I don't *know*," whined the pastor, catching the irony of her uncertainty. "The scripture for Sunday is about choosing life. I'm so indecisive I can't even choose how I want you to help me."

The waitress appeared with the Wise Old Woman's order and filled the pastor's coffee cup. As she reached for the jam, the Wise

Old Woman said, "Tell me about the scripture texts for tomorrow, my dear."

"Well," the pastor began, "the Hebrew scripture is from the book of Deuteronomy. Moses is 120 years old. He has led his people out of slavery in Egypt. He has kept them alive and safe through forty years in the wilderness, interpreted God's gift of law to them, and led them to the very edge of the promised land. Now, he is getting ready to die. He knows he won't be going with them into the land of Canaan. The scripture is part of his last sermon. He reminds the people of their covenant with God. He summarizes: 'Choose life!' Choosing life means loving God and holding fast to the covenant, the Torah.

"In Matthew," the pastor continued, "Jesus is interpreting the Torah. People have become legalistic about it and are fighting over interpretations of it. Jesus talks about the spirit of the law and fulfilling the law. He summarizes: 'Love God and neighbor as yourself.' Then, Jesus talks about offerings. He says our relationships with our neighbors are more important to God than our offerings."

The Wise Old Woman listened carefully. She knew if she listened until the pastor ran out of words and kept silent, in that silence the pastor often came to new insight. At this moment, the pastor seemed to be heading in the insight direction.

"It is interesting, Wise Old Woman. Moses doesn't list the Ten Commandments and then say, 'Choose *right!*' He talks about the hearts going astray from God and says, 'Choose *life!*' And, Jesus doesn't list all the laws regarding offerings and say, 'Make yourself pure, give your first fruits, bring God at least ten percent of what you have.' Jesus says, 'The gift God wants is a pure heart.' Jesus implies one finds a pure heart through whole relationships. If we've done something to hurt our neighbor, we're told to get that cleared up before we offer our heart to God. The issue is not so much choosing between right and wrong as much as choosing between loving and unloving."

The Wise Old Woman did her own summarizing. "Hmmmm. Moses says, 'Choose life.' Jesus says, 'Choose love.' "

"That's essentially it," agreed the pastor.

"That'll preach, won't it?" asked the Wise Old Woman, hopefully. She wiped her lips with her napkin, having long ago finished her muffin as the pastor talked.

"Yes," agreed the pastor with some hesitation, "but what does it *look* like to choose life or choose love?"

"Oh, now you want *specifics*?"

The pastor grinned. She realized how much she longs for clear answers. She also realized that in all the thousands of decisions she makes, she most often makes choices without even thinking. If she does think about her choices, she sometimes becomes even more indecisive. Is she choosing *Life* or choosing *Death*? Is she choosing *Love* or choosing *Evil*? She doesn't often get clear answers or have the assurance she's making clear choices.

For instance, she thought about the way she spends her money and her time. Friday, her day off, after she talked with her D.S., she bought a book on word processing called *AmiPro for Dummies*. She was determined to learn how to use a computer. By buying the book and sitting for hours at the computer, will she be choosing life or death? Will her skill, provided she gets it, bring more compassion into being, or less? Wouldn't the $20.00 she paid for the manual be better spent on diapers for children at Women's Horizons? Would the time spent in front of the computer screen be better spent in volunteer work at the Sharing Center?

As if she knew the pastor was struggling with indecision, the waitress *chose* that moment to bring over the coffee pot and ask the pastor if she wanted a refill.

"I can't *decide*!" the pastor groaned. "I LOVE coffee. It's bad for me. If I say 'yes' I'm choosing both life and death!"

The waitress, shocked and confused by the pastor's outburst, hurried away.

"Oh, Wise Old Woman," agonized the pastor, "I think the people gathered on Sunday have some of the same difficulty I have trying to choose life and choose love. Whether big decisions or small ones, they make choices all week long: time, money, activities, family events, medical conditions, what to eat, what to wear ... We're not too different from the people of Moses' and Jesus' time. We know the laws. We know the commandments backward and forward. We can even recite memory verses proclaiming the Good News. We want to choose life and love. The question is: 'How do we *do* it?' "

For several moments the Wise Old Woman sat in silence, looking thoughtful and wise. Then she said, "What do you want to have happen Sunday morning, my dear?"

"I want for folks, myself included, to be persuaded to choose life. In our big decisions and little ones, I want us to choose love. I want hearts to be changed, mine included. I want to be more caring. I want neighbors who have grudges with each other to be reconciled. I want offerings to be made from hearts overflowing with life and love."

"Hmmmm. That's quite a list and none of it is exclusively your job, my dear," the Wise Old Woman pointed out, quietly.

"It isn't?" replied the pastor, knowing the answer even as she asked the question.

"No. Changed hearts and changed decisions are God's department, the work of the Holy Spirit.

"Remember Moses? He is at the end of his life. He has spent at least forty years with these people. He has led them, prayed with them and for them, interceded to God on their behalf, suffered with them, and agonized because of them. Here he is, 120 years old, and still desperate for them to choose life. He couldn't force them to do it.

"Jesus couldn't force love either. Until after his death and resurrection, many of his words just made people mad. His words still expose our need to choose between life and death, love or evil. His words got him killed and still cause trouble for his followers."

Looking the pastor straight in the eye, the Wise Old Woman asked, "Do you think *your* words are supposed to be more persuasive than either Jesus or Moses?

"If folks really want to choose life and choose love, they must call on God's grace for themselves. They will need to read, study, pray, and work with the power the Holy Spirit gives them. You, too, my dear," added the Wise Old Woman. "And, the Holy Spirit is even responsible for the *desire* to choose life and love."

The pastor, whose ego was slightly bruised, was beginning to catch on. "Are you saying I really don't have to do *anything* tomorrow?"

"Well, yes and no," laughed the Wise Old Woman, sounding rather indecisive herself. "Why don't you trust God's grace and power to be present and then see what you choose to say?"

With those words, the sun broke through the clouds, shone full force on the Wise Old Woman's rhinestone initials, and lit up the Taste Of Wisconsin with shimmering insight. The pastor decided to thank her friend and have another cup of coffee, but when the glittering faded away, the Wise Old Woman was gone.